mind games

Matthew Paul Turner

advice, stories, and
truth for thinking free

MiND
gAMes

TYNDALE HOUSE PUBLISHERS, INC., CAROL STREAM, ILLINOIS

Visit Tyndale's exciting Web site at www.tyndale.com

TYNDALE and Tyndale's quill logo are registered trademarks of Tyndale House Publishers, Inc.

Mind Games: Advice, Stories, and Truth for Thinking Free

Designed by Stephen Vosloo

Some of the names, places, and specific events in this book have been changed to protect the identity of an individual. Any familiar similarities found in stories, places, and events are coincidental.

Scripture quotations marked NLT are taken from the *Holy Bible,* New Living Translation, copyright © 1996. Used by permission of Tyndale House Publishers, Inc., Carol Stream, Illinois 60188. All rights reserved.

Scripture quotations marked NIV are taken from the *Holy Bible,* New International Version®. NIV®. Copyright © 1973, 1978, 1984 by International Bible Society. Used by permission of Zondervan. All rights reserved.

Scripture quotations marked "The Message" are taken from *THE MESSAGE.* Copyright © 1993, 1994, 1995, 1996, 2000, 2001, 2002. Used by permission of NavPress Publishing Group.

Scripture quotations marked KJV are taken from the *Holy Bible,* King James Version.

Library of Congress Cataloging-in-Publication Data
Turner, Matthew Paul, date.
Mind games : advice, stories, and truth for thinking free / Matthew Paul Turner.
   p. cm.
  ISBN-13: 978-1-4143-0558-5 (sc)
  ISBN-10: 1-4143-0558-3 (sc)
1. Christian life. 2. Thought and thinking—Religious aspects—Christianity. 3. Common fallacies. I. Title.
BV4501.3.T85 2006
248.4—dc22   2005034943

Printed in the United States of America

12 11 10 09 08 07 06
7   6   5   4   3   2   1

*For my father, **Walter Virgil Turner**—an honest and faithful man who has taught me how to think with integrity and grace.*

brain dump

I would like to thank . . .

My beloved family; my family-in-law, the Schims; Daniel Eagan; Ken, Carol, Ron, Stephen, Travis, Jamie, Karen, and Dave at Tyndale House Publishers—thank you for treating me like a best-selling author; my friends—you know who you are; my beautiful wife, Jessica; and God Almighty for peace of mind.

"These are the words in my mouth; these are what I chew on and pray. Accept them when I place them on the morning altar, O God, my Altar-Rock, God, Priest-of-My-Altar" (Psalm 19:14, "The Message").

thoughts

Your thoughts can make you believe or make you doubt. They can be true or false. They can lead you toward a healthy lifestyle or steal away your ability to live a fulfilled life. Perhaps most powerfully, thoughts have the ability to free you, or they can enslave you inside the worst cage of all . . . yourself.

Journal Entry: SEPTEMBER 23, 1998

Last night I couldn't sleep. I just tossed and turned all night long. Yet as much as I couldn't sleep, I can't find enough energy to get out of bed either. I think I might be depressed. . . . I hate feeling depressed. I feel depressed often these days. I've felt all this before; depression is something that, once you've experienced it, you never forget it.

I believe God has placed inside each of us a desire for intimate passion, soulful purpose, and mind-boggling potential. Yet too often we let our minds (or the way we think) get in the way of all that. We let our poor thinking dictate how we are going to live. We invest poorly in our minds, so we get a poor return on our investment. In short, we play mind games with ourselves.

I've played mind games for most of my adult life. One day a couple of years ago, I woke up and decided I was going to stop cold turkey. No more playing the games that had so often left me feeling depressed, anxious, obsessed, alone, fearful, codependent, and paranoid. I'm no shrink or theologian, and I will not pretend to be, but I've learned over the past several years what God can do with the human mind. And I'm living proof that he can use just about any type of mind for his purpose and glory. The book you're now holding, Mind Games, *is one part my story and one part the lessons I've learned about my mind and how I cannot survive without thinking free—and neither can you.*

I coined the term freethinking *to describe a mind that is free of game playing, free of bondage, free of self-absorption. A mind in pursuit of being surrendered to the passions and dreams of Jesus is truly free. I've often had to learn this the hard way on my journey of faith. But I've come to realize that the more I surrender, the more I am able to be free from the bondage of worry, anxiety, and depression. It's not like I don't ever feel those things; I do, but they no longer define who I am. They don't lock me up in a cage. They don't control me. My pursuit of being dependent on Jesus sets me free from that cage.*

Reality brings challenges into our lives that can send us into mental tailspins. I've been there. You've probably been there, too. But no matter whether it's depression or anxiety or codependence or anger or lack of confidence or fear that cripples our ability to think free, God can heal it. That's what freethinking is all about—finding freedom and healing. And we all need it, no matter what our stories entail. . . .

possession

POSSESSION IS A MIND GAME DRIVEN AND ROOTED IN FEAR. IT IS
FEAR THAT KEEPS YOU FROM LETTING GOD POSSESS YOUR MIND.
YOU'RE AFRAID OF WHAT HE'LL DO WITH IT. YOU LIKE THINKING WHAT
YOU WANT TO THINK BECAUSE IT FEELS LIKE FREEDOM. THE ONLY
THING IS, YOU DON'T REALLY HAVE POSSESSION OF YOUR OWN MIND
ANYWAY, AND THE ABILITY TO THINK WHAT YOU WANT ISN'T EXACTLY
FREEDOM. . . .

Journal Entry: AUGUST 8, 1998

*A couple of days ago, I met someone who reminded me
of a simple truth about God and his desire to have my mind.
It's just so hard letting him have it.*

A few years ago, I visited a therapist.

I had never gone to a therapist before—at least I had never
paid for therapy, and the person I had seen was a good friend. It's

not that I deemed myself too healthy for therapy. Believe me; the opposite was true. I was pretty convinced that a therapist would be a delightful bonus to my already Christian-advice-laden lifestyle.

When you're a Christian who has been saturated for more than twenty years with advice from other Christians, therapy's almost a requirement. But up until that moment, I had always stopped short of even thinking about visiting a therapist. Why? Simply put, I was afraid of what people might think of me if they knew I was *seeing* someone, *really* "seeing someone." And at that time, this kind of seeing someone was up there with the committing-adultery kind of seeing someone.

But I went through with it.

When Dr. Jane Stevens walked into the waiting room from her office, I was quietly but anxiously praying to myself.

She looked nothing like I'd expected. When I'd made the appointment, her phone voice led me to believe she would be tall, thin, and probably pretty attractive. Don't ask me why, but some people have voices that say, "I'm a pretty person." But Dr. Stevens turned out to look nothing like the picture my imagination had created. She was short and stocky, with sandy red hair. And by the looks of things, she didn't care much for the styles of 2001. Heck, she didn't care much for the styles of *1981*. In fact, this forty-something therapist looked as if she had just jumped out of *1961*. Her hair was fixed with more bobby pins than any woman under the age of seventy-five should own. I couldn't help but stare. It seemed like she was trying to keep something constrained up there—as if her hair were in a straitjacket.

I hope she treats her patients better than her hair.

On the other hand, her voice was throaty, smooth, and enticing.

"Matthew, why don't you start by telling me why you came to visit me today."

"Well," I said nervously, "I'm having some issues with anxiety— and honestly, I am probably a little depressed. Oh, and I've got some issues with my past."

Dr. Stevens was taking notes.

"I'm also pretty sure I have a codependent personality," I continued. "At least my mother thinks so."

Dr. Stevens was nodding.

"And I'm perhaps a little neurotic, always overcome with guilt, and probably still trying to outfox some spiritual abuse I experienced as a child."

I stopped for a second and reviewed my mental checklist. "I think that's it."

Dr. Stevens looked at me intently. "I'm curious, Matthew; can you tell me about the spiritual abuse?"

"The spiritual abuse began when I was five," I said. "That's when I asked Jesus to come into my heart and be my Savior. But before I get to that . . ."

The whole time I chatted, Dr. Stevens hardly looked up at me. As I spoke, she took notes on a large yellow legal pad.

I went on to tell her my entire life story. I started at the very beginning, at least as far back as I could remember. I told her how my little town of Chestertown, Maryland, had been a delightful place to grow up. Quaint little streets, large cornfields, steamed blue crabs in the summertime—I told her everything.

Knowing that therapists were sometimes able to tell when you were exaggerating, I made sure to be as convincing as I could possibly be. And I think she believed me, too, when I talked lovingly, graciously, and sickeningly sweetly about my parents and my three sisters.

"Sure, they were far from perfect, but they always loved me. They were *never* the problem," I said emphatically. But then I began talking about my church.

Dr. Stevens seemed to know exactly what I was talking about. She nodded her head, rolled her eyes, and said, "Hmm" at just the right moments. I don't know whether or not she followed Jesus, but she certainly asked what seemed like a thousand questions about my Christian upbringing. Her eyes got big when I told her that two of my teachers from the Christian school I attended had committed suicide. She cringed a bit when I talked about the guilt I felt every time I did anything that was deemed wrong in the eyes of the church.

I stumbled over my come-to-Jesus story for thirty minutes.

Finally, she looked at me and said in that misleading sultry voice of hers, "Matthew, that's quite a story, but I think I can help you. Everything I've heard from you today tells me you're fighting something inside."

She was getting deep. Her words were pulling at heartstrings that I didn't know I had. Was I fighting God? Was I trying to keep something from him?

Dr. Stevens continued, "As a child, you looked to the church and your family to help you fit in. That kept you sheltered for a long time. As a college student, you went more toward sexual freedom and partying. But you still came up empty. . . . Matthew, your life is a puzzle, and you're still busy looking for some of the pieces."

On the outside, I kept quiet and appeared interested. But inside, I fought her every word. *I am a Jesus follower,* I thought. *When you follow Jesus, you only need one puzzle piece. And that's* his *piece.* As I sat there, I fed myself every piece of Christian jargon I could remember: *I shouldn't be here; this was a bad idea.*

Despite my thoughts, I went back to see Dr. Stevens the very next week. When she walked out to welcome me into her office again, the first thing I noticed was her new haircut. Although the bobby pins were still there, they didn't seem to be working quite as hard.

"So, Matthew, today we're going to do an exercise that I call *intervention*," Dr. Stevens said.

Her mellifluous voice again soothed my soul. I wanted to bottle it up and take it home with me so I could open it when I was having trouble sleeping.

"I am going to ask you to close your eyes," she continued, "and I want you to think of a time, any time in your past, when you felt you were being abused—spiritually, mentally, emotionally. It doesn't matter."

All of what she had just rambled on about scared me. *Close my eyes? Think of a time?* It all sounded a little too much like a rerun episode of *Dr. Phil.*

"So, go ahead," she murmured. "Close your eyes."

I closed my eyes. I closed them tight. As soon as I did, shapes, colors, and spots—all very bright and vivid—formed on the inside of my eyelids.

"I want you to think of one instance in your childhood where you felt abused. It might be something that occurred in the Christian school that you attended. It might be something that one of the pastors said to you. . . ."

With my eyes closed and Dr. Stevens's voice feeling like sweet, sensual whispers in my ear, I searched my memory for an occurrence that had hurt me or left me feeling deflated or enslaved. Surprisingly, this was more difficult than I thought it would be. Because so much of the pain and frustration was brought on through my church life as a whole, it was hard to put my finger on one event.

"Are you there yet, Matthew?" asked Dr. Stevens.

"I think so."

"Well, take your time."

"OK, I think I'm there."

"Tell me about the moment you're thinking of right now."

"I'm fourteen years old," I began, still feeling very uncomfortable with this psychic exercise, but in the interests of mental health I forged ahead with as much confidence as I could muster. "I'm sitting in the front row of an Algebra 2 class. My desk is piled high with paper and books and homework and folders. It's one of those desks where the table is attached to the chair with a bar. It's a little wobbly, probably because it's old. . . . Anyway, in the middle of class, two 'friends' pushed my desk forward so that the table hit the floor. . . ."

As uncomfortable as this whole experience was making me feel, as much as I was trying to protect myself from feeling anything at all, I began to experience something in that moment, something I hadn't expected. As hard as it was for me to understand, sitting in that moment I really felt like I was fourteen again, being picked on in that math class.

"Books, papers, and everything else on my desk fell and scattered on the floor around me. My face flew forward and hit the edge of the desk and I slipped out of the seat and onto the floor. I didn't get hurt, really—there was no blood—but it was painful and humiliating. . . ."

As I shared that story, I could feel my face getting pale, and my gut stirred with anger and emotion. A lot of junk that I had been feeling for years began to overwhelm me. I could feel a couple of tears forming in my eyes.

"As soon as the noise of the desk hitting the floor rang out through the classroom, everyone belted out in mass amounts of laughter. Some people were barreled over in hysteria. Even those who normally didn't laugh at stuff like that snickered. The teacher stood up, and to my frustration, he laughed, too. But you see, Dr. Stevens, that's not the whole story. . . ."

I leaned back into the couch, my eyes still tightly shut, trying to get more comfortable.

"From the time I was four years old, I had to wear a brace around my entire back because of scoliosis. The brace made movement difficult, and it was uncomfortable to bend over because the brace covered three inches of my butt in the back and covered my private area in the front. . . ."

Dr. Stevens never said a word the entire time I shared my story. I guess she simply watched me. Maybe she was writing stuff down on that tablet of hers.

"I instantly began to pick up everything that had fallen off my desk. Everyone was still laughing, and not one person helped me. . . ."

I looked up at Dr. Stevens and a couple more tears rolled down my cheeks. I felt a little foolish crying about something that had happened many years before.

"That's one of probably a hundred stories I could remember that evoke similar emotions and anger in me," I said frankly.

Time was up. But my time of learning and understanding had just begun. I discovered I had been holding on for dear life to everything that caused me pain. I was holding on to my past. I was holding on to guilt. I was holding on to anger. I was holding everything tightly in my memory, in the deepest parts of my mind. For the first time, I could see how everything I was holding on to was crippling my ability to think clearly and free. It wasn't an easy fix, but over time, God made it clear what needed to be done.

He wanted my mind, how I thought about stuff, the junk I had filled it with—*he wanted it all.*

confessions of a strange mind

when i was nine years old, i walked out of a church function upset because no one was eating my mother's green bean casserole. by the look of complete sadness written all over my face, you would have thought that the church had publicly ridiculed my mom for making such a disgusting dish. but that's how my mind was interpreting the situation. everyone was eating all of miss janet's potato salad, miss kitty's macaroni and cheese, and miss pam's fruit salad, leaving my mom's dish without one scoop missing. there might as well have been a sign next to my mom's dish that read, "this casserole sucks; do not eat." to be honest, i didn't even like my mom's green bean casserole. but, more importantly, i didn't want my mom's feelings to be hurt when she realized that no one was eating her potluck dish. so i went through the food line six different times, took a large helping of the green beans, and proceeded to run into the bathroom and throw it in the trash. yes, i felt a little guilty for misleading my mom, but the guilt seemed well worth it because she went home thinking her potluck had been a hit.

God knows every thought that flashes through our minds. That's scary to me. He knows about the dirty thoughts. He knows about the dreamy thoughts I have about life. He knows which of my thoughts make me feel guilty; he knows the ones that make me feel free. He knows the questions my mind asks. But even with all that he knows about my mind, God never once thinks about trying to run away or leaving me alone. Although, I must admit, sometimes it certainly *feels* like he has.

Surprisingly, my mind doesn't scare God. He simply wants me to know what it's like to think free. He believes that only in his hands can my mind begin to dance like he created it to dance.

God is not surprised by the influence our minds have on our daily situations. In fact, he has a bird's-eye view of how our minds affect our work, relationships, families, sex lives, entertainment choices, ministry possibilities, spiritual choices, and so much more.

God knows that our minds play a passionately vigorous role in determining who we are as individuals.

Most people, at least the ones I know, are quite aware that the way we think can either make us or break us as people. That's why God wants to be involved in how we think. He deems it necessary to have control of our minds because he knows that we can't even begin to think good thoughts and make good decisions without his involvement, without his wisdom guiding our minds on a continuing basis.

In so many of our circumstances, we don't realize how much God desires to renew and give life to our minds. We think we can do it on our own. We think we don't need God scuttling around inside our heads. We think our minds are fine without his involvement. But we're not fine without him.

It took me a long time before I learned this truth.

I can't tell you how many times God has asked me to give him my mind—by my count, at least thirty-seven times. Every time he's come to me with this request, he's taken a different approach. Sometimes he used his well-loved and much-talked-about gentle whisper—you know, the soft voice of sanity that was barely audible over the music booming through my headphones. Sometimes he'd come to me with a boisterous proclamation—loud, clear, and obvious—but I still didn't listen. Not very often, but once in a while, God would come in the form of a miracle (think Moses' burning bush experience), except in my case, nothing was burning but the brain cells I used to try to ignore him. No doubt, I've learned the hard way that God doesn't let our ignorance and evasiveness dissuade him from trying to get our attention. No matter what new excuses I came up with, he was always extremely persistent in trying to get me to surrender control of my mind.

Around the time that I turned twenty, I became aware that God was asking me to surrender my mind to him. The first time he asked, I just laughed at him. The second time he asked, I pretended to not hear him. The third time, he sent the Holy Spirit to do his dirty work, and I ended battling mono for a month (long story, but true). OK, so I'm not sure whether the mono and God's Spirit had anything to do with each other, but to me it felt that way.

Every time God asked me for my mind, I had some type of verbal or visceral response. I was quick with the big excuses for why I didn't want to surrender my mind. Little did I know that it's in God's nature to intervene as much as he believes is necessary to get his kids exactly where he wants them to be. Truthfully, sometimes I found his persistence to be annoying and obnoxious; yet at the same time, there were definitely times when I felt grateful that he continued to invest in me. But regardless of my feelings about his persistence, I was clear and up-front with him. I told him every time that I had made a conscious decision not to give up my mind without a fight.

To my surprise, my antics didn't alarm God.

He didn't even flinch.

He simply kept reminding me of his desire for my life to be complete. And he knew that completion was not possible without my mind being safely in his hands.

Let me get one thing straight, though: God hated my mind games. He was patient with me, but he hated the fact that I was running from him. And I soon learned that he was willing to use *anybody* and *anything* to gain possession of my mind.

One of God's "little reminders" came in 1998. A group of friends and I went on a weekend trip to Kings Dominion amusement park, outside of Richmond, Virginia. The six of us got up early that morning, piled into my friend's minivan, and ventured off to have a day of fun.

When I was a kid, amusement parks were always a lot of fun. But as I got older, I began to realize that they also wore me out, made me sick, and were somewhat stressful.

After about six hours of running from rides to attractions to games to places with air-conditioning, I felt as if I had spent the day doing hard labor, and I was pretty much ready to go home. But not my friends. They were just getting warmed up. By the time three o'clock in the afternoon rolled around, I had decided to take some time to relax on a bench directly beneath one of the most popular roller coasters in the park. It seemed like a prime location for one of my favorite hobbies, which is people watching.

By this time, the line for the roller coaster was ninety minutes long. Nevertheless, hundreds of people walked past me on their way to the end of the line. Fat people. Skinny people. Pretty people. Ugly people. Peculiar people. Grungy people. I sat with my five-dollar blue cotton candy in one hand and an extra-large orange soda in the other, watching all kinds of people make the decision to wait for an hour-and-a-half in the hot August heat for a thirty-five-second joyride.

About fifteen minutes later, a large, cheerful, middle-aged

woman with lots of stuff sat down next to me. She had two diaper bags, a stroller, a couple of toys, and a cooler with her. She looked kind of like a suburbanite version of a bag lady. But despite her frazzled appearance, she was still full of energy. Seemingly eager to chat, she didn't hesitate to speak up as soon as she had gotten herself settled.

"Hello, I'm Patricia Black," she proclaimed loudly, looking me straight in the eye. Her gaze was so sharp and strong that it felt as if she were trying to stare a hole right through me.

"Nice to meet you, Patricia. Are you waiting for your children to get on the roller coaster?"

It was a rhetorical question, sort of like saying, "How're you doing?" as you pass someone on the sidewalk. What I was really hoping was that she would leave me alone so I could go back to watching people. God must have known I was impatient, because suddenly I felt him nudge me and say, "Shut up and listen. I sent her." But even hearing God's voice in my heart didn't make me want to sit and talk to this lady.

"Yep, they'll be in that line for at least an hour or so," she bellowed with a grin, her Virginian accent coming through a bit. "How about you? What's your name, young man?"

"Matthew," I said quietly, still hoping for a way out of this sure-to-be-long conversation.

"Good to know you, Matthew. Why aren't you standing in line for the ride?"

"Oh, I'm exhausted; I've already been on this ride once today. I told my friends to go on without me."

I turned my attention back to the passing crowds. But despite my best efforts to ignore her, Patricia Black continued to talk. And, boy, did she like to talk—a lot. Not that I was trying real hard, but I barely got a word in. She told me about her family (three kids, two cats, a dog, and a husband); her childhood (she was one of seven poor kids born to a miner and his doting, homely wife—her words, not mine); her job (she worked as a counselor at a children's mental hospital in Roanoke); and her life lessons learned (too many to mention here).

After a twenty-minute conversation (if *conversation* is the right word for our very one-sided interaction), I noticed something strangely wonderful about Mrs. Patricia Black. She loved to retell her father's analogies about life.

"I *love* roller coasters," she said boldly. "My daddy always told me that life was just like one big roller coaster ride. It's often full of hard climbs, fast descents, and quick twists and turns. But then whenever Daddy told me that, he would always grin and say, 'But if you hold on tight and let it take you where it's going to take you, it's always a fun ride.'"

"That's an interesting theory," I said, smiling. I was becoming more and more interested and tolerant of what she had to say.

"Daddy had lots of good theories. I wish I had listened to him more," she said.

"Well, you must have listened to some of them because you seem to be very happy," I said. "Not many people are really happy these days." In my mind, I was still contemplating whether or not I agreed with her father's roller coaster theory.

"Well, you know, Matthew, my daddy once told me that if I wanted to be happy, I needed to keep my mind clean from all the junk this world tries to give you." (Well, she didn't actually say *junk*.)

"Daddy always said that God wants my mind—that it's got to be his. I didn't understand any of that when he first said it to me, but I figure it means we need to keep our minds on the good and true things of life. Whatever we put into our minds always ends up pouring out into the rest of what we do."

I was silenced (which honestly doesn't happen very often). God had managed to find me again, and this time he used a cursing stranger to try to get my attention. Patricia was right. God does want possession of our minds. And it's for our own good.

Consider Philippians 4:8: "Fix your thoughts on what is true and honorable and right. Think about things that are pure and lovely and admirable. Think about things that are excellent and worthy of praise" (NLT).

{
MY DEFINITION: possession

Something that's not important until you have to give it up to somebody else.

Conversation with my therapist-slash-friend

I'm just gonna be frank with you and recommend that you find a therapist-slash-friend. Everybody needs one. Let's face it: Who doesn't love—and need—a little free counseling every now and then? My therapist-slash-friend's name is Bill. We're still friends.

"Am I crazy, Bill?"

"Do you think you're crazy, Matthew?"

Silence.

"No really, answer the question, Matthew—do you think you're crazy?"

"No, I don't think so," I said, half expecting him to laugh me out of my chair.

"Yeah, I don't think you are either."

"You don't think I'm crazy either?"

"Gosh no, you're not crazy. You just don't always think right."

"So, what's the difference between someone who is crazy and someone who simply doesn't think right, Bill?"

"The man who is crazy gets a bill for a hundred bucks from me every week."

"Oh."

While I was attending college, it was always one of my goals to try to get to know my professors on a more personal basis. I did this for two reasons (and honestly, both reasons were kind of selfish). First of all, when I had a relationship with a professor, it was much more difficult for him or her to fail me. Also, professors usually had a great deal of insight about life that I could learn from. This strategy proved quite helpful throughout my college career.

One such relationship was with a sociology professor named Gerald Grant. Professor Grant wasn't even a real professor, just an adjunct who taught only one evening class a week. His nine-to-five gig was as a counselor for troubled kids at a local kids' jail in Nashville. He was a God-follower working with kids who broke the law, got caught, and were serving time in juvenile detention. In our class, he was very open about the situations he encountered. He couldn't mention names, of course, but he could talk about the kids' experiences, their search for healing, and how most of them were creating patterns they would follow for the rest of their lives. One afternoon, I met Professor Grant for coffee. Afterward, he took me on a private tour of the detention center, where most of his days were spent trying to get to the heart of these kids' issues.

"This is where most of them spend their days," he said, showing me a large room decorated so plainly that I felt depression setting in as soon as I entered through the gray metal doors. "Although some kids are restricted from this area, most of them are allowed to roam freely here."

"How do you help these kids?" I asked as we sat down at one of the tables in the deserted recreation room.

"Each kid is different, Matthew," he said with a hint of intrigue and a smile. "Each kid has had his or her own experiences. You can't lump them together into one megatheory."

"Then how can you even begin to help each kid's individual needs if the kids are all so different?"

"Each child computes his or her past differently. It's my job to help them make peace with their past issues and help them not let what has happened in the past affect their present situations or their futures."

"Do you get to talk about God with these kids?" I asked.

"I do, but only indirectly. I'd get fired if I spoke too plainly. But this facility is a little more open-minded to spiritual help than many other places I've worked."

"So, is there a core problem that each of these kids faces?"

"Yep, it's the same problem you and I face in our lives."

"Really? How so?" I asked.

"In order to really be helped, these kids have to surrender their minds to God. You and I have to do the same. Our minds are pointless without God's direction. We can't even begin to think good thoughts without his involvement. Yes, these kids have endured horrible experiences, but the truth is that God can take these broken minds and use them."

Professor Grant laid it out for me as clearly and concisely as he could. Still, I ignored God's little nudge.

But my days of ignoring God were numbered.

On January 20, 2002, I broke a girl's heart.

OK, so I didn't just break it; I pretty much ripped it out of her chest and jumped up and down on it. The whole situation was really rather ugly, and to be honest, it's embarrassing for me to talk about it even now. But if I'm going to share it, I need to back up and start at the beginning.

It was a chilly October day and I was talking to my best friend on the phone. He had called me with some exciting news. He was getting engaged! *Yippee!* I could practically see his happy grin over the phone. It was one of those I-am-so-excited-I'm-in-love-that-I-could-scream kinds of grins that make the unmarried and not-yet-in-love person want to run to the nearest bathroom to vomit. If you're single, you probably know the feeling. I tried not to let on about the whole "gag reflex" thing, of course. So, instead of running to the bathroom, I mustered enough proper etiquette to say all the things that best friends are supposed to say when their buddy is getting ready to pop the big question to the girl of his dreams.

"Gosh, I'm excited for you."

"Whatever I can do to help with the wedding, you can count on me."

"You guys are going to be so happy together."

A-a-a-u-c-c-c-h!

Honestly, I couldn't get off the phone fast enough. So, I made up some I'm-getting-ready-to-walk-out-the-front-door-I-should-let-you-go excuse to say good-bye. After I hung up the phone, my mind went into a state of panic.

I instantly felt very single and very alone and very much like a complete loser. Honestly, you would have thought I had just aged ten years, gained forty-two pounds, and gone bankrupt during that ten-minute phone conversation with my friend. Consequently, a downward-spiraling dialogue began in my head:

"*Is there something seriously wrong with me? All of my friends are pairing up with spouses like they're getting ready to board Noah's ark. And I don't have anyone to get on the boat with.*"

"*I know, Matthew; you're getting old, and quite honestly, you're not as good looking as you once were. By the way, have you gained weight?*"

"*Just so you know, you're not helping me feel any better.*"

"*I didn't know I was here to make you feel better.*"

"*Hey, maybe I should just put myself out there and start dating again. That's it! I should just throw myself into a committed relationship.*"

"*Oh yeah, that's a great idea; you should definitely do all of what you just said.*"

And that's exactly what I did. I decided that day (in about thirty seconds, I might add) that I was just going to commit myself to the next girl who showed any interest in me whatsoever. Heck, I didn't even know who that lucky girl was going to be. But if she was the least bit interested, I was going for it. I was going to dive in deep and make that relationship work.

Finding that potential companion didn't really take all that long. An old friend and I had been hanging out a little bit. In fact, she made the first move—which I took as a sign from God. True to my vow, I crossed the Jordan River, hoping to find the Promised Land.

Within a short four weeks, she was in love with me, and we were buying each other expensive Christmas gifts, exciting our parents with "this is the one" conversations, and portraying the perfectly happy couple in front of all our friends and family. As weird as this all now seems to me (and no doubt you, too), I honestly wanted the relationship to work. I wanted to love her. I wanted her to be my wife. I wanted to live happily ever after. I wanted all of these things, but after seven weeks of complete abandonment to all reason and sanity, I panicked—again.

The conversation in my head began again:

"You don't love this girl, Matthew! You think she's nice, you think she's cute and has a nice family, but you don't love her."

"Yeah, but maybe I can make it work. She does have a nice family. My parents like her. She's easygoing. I might be able to spend forever like this."

"You are a screwed-up mess, Matthew. You're in love with the idea of being in love, but you're not in love. Who are you kidding? You can't make this thing work. This is a train wreck getting ready to happen. This is all a figment of your pathetic imagination."

"Are you saying that I should just put an end to this? But I don't want to hurt her."

"Yes, without a doubt you need to put an end to this. Matthew, you're eventually going to hurt her anyway. It might as well be now."

"OK."

As quickly as my head had fallen in love with the concept of a bona fide commitment, I decided this wasn't the way to go. So I called it off. I blamed it on myself. I gave her the "it's me, not you" excuse. I told her I had head problems that I couldn't explain. Which, honestly, was true; I couldn't explain what was going on in my head.

After the bad good-bye to a good friend whom I had led on, after the thirty-seven times that God had asked for my mind, after a lump the size of Texas had formed inside my gut—that's when I realized I couldn't take it anymore. I didn't want to keep fighting. I told God he could have my mind.

The very next day, I got up out of bed and then down on my knees and cried my way through this prayer: "God, you can have my mind. You can have all of me. I want to be yours—all yours. Possess my mind and use it how you see fit. I cannot do this in my own strength and wisdom any longer. Please help me."

OK, so that was it, right? Not quite. I still have to get up and pray that prayer almost every day of my life—sometimes two or three times a day, sometimes more than that. Giving God possession of your mind—allowing him to control your thoughts—is an ongoing battle.

independence

NO ONE GOES THROUGH LIFE WITHOUT PLAYING THE MIND GAME OF INDEPENDENCE AT LEAST ONCE. USUALLY, THE GAME IS ONGOING. THE HUMAN NEED TO CONTROL LIFE ONLY FUELS THE THOUGHT THAT INDEPENDENCE IS ATTAINABLE. BUT ON YOUR OWN YOU'RE WEAK, VULNERABLE, AND DISCONNECTED FROM GOD'S DREAM FOR YOUR LIFE. INDEPENDENCE MIGHT SEEM LIKE A POWERFUL EXISTENCE, BUT ONCE THE DISGUISE GETS LIFTED, YOU REALIZE THAT YOU ACTUALLY HAVEN'T BEEN LIVING A LIFE OF FREEDOM; YOU'VE BEEN LOCKED INSIDE MERE CONFORMITY.

During the summer of 1999, God came to me with a simple request. (OK, the truth: It wasn't simple to me at all; it was tragic.) The request came at a time when I was probably the happiest and most contented I had ever been. But God seemingly wasn't concerned with my contentment when he asked me to move from my comfortable home in Maryland to the great metropolis of Washington, D.C., for a job. I was less than thrilled about saying yes and taking

God up on his offer. Like I said, I had finally gotten to a place in my life where I felt settled in and connected where I was living. I had a job. My family was close. I liked my church. And honestly, I didn't want to leave the sweetness of my comfort zone. I had control of my life and was doing quite well, thank you. But God had other plans for my life. Plans I didn't understand. Plans I didn't want to understand.

Because of my quandary with God, I decided to talk to a pastor friend about my situation to see if he could shed any new light on my dilemma. My friend is from the suburbs of London, and he embodies every characteristic of a true British gentleman, except good people skills. So, not surprisingly, he had some very quick and frank words for me.

"Matthew, I can't argue with God for you," he said in no uncertain terms. "That's not how God works. And to be honest, it's not how I work either." He paused for a long moment and took a deep breath. "Frankly, I don't mind giving you my opinion, but ultimately it's between you and God."

"I realize that," I said, finding it rather difficult not to mimic his annoyingly precise English accent. "I'm not trying to get you to fight my battle for me—but can't you help me figure this out? Don't you think that if this request is truly from God, he would at least give me a little bit of a desire to make the move to northern Virginia?"

"That's hogwash, Matthew. God doesn't work that way, either. I think that's one huge misconception about God. He sometimes expects our desires to change in order to be in line with what he has willed for us. That's not always the easiest thing to do, but it's what he expects. If God has told you to move to northern Virginia, you need to fall in line and make that your desire."

I stared at him blankly, thinking about his use of the phrase "fall in line" and how legalistic it sounded. I hated legalism then, and I still hate it now.

"Matthew, can I be really honest with you?"

"Sure," I said somewhat hesitantly.

"It sounds like you're fighting with God over something much bigger than just moving to Virginia. What are you keeping from him that he wants? What is he trying to get a hold of in you that you're not willing to give him?"

I just continued to stare at him. My mind was rushing from thought to thought to thought, trying to figure out how in the world my British friend knew this much about my life. He didn't know me all that well. I figured it had to be one of those Holy Spirit thingies that at that point I didn't understand.

"Well, actually, you might be on to something," I said, slowly and hesitantly. "Lately, I've felt very disconnected from God—like we're not on the same page or something. My prayer time is off. I've been struggling with my thought life. I feel depressed and anxious. I probably need a little therapy." (I laughed; my friend didn't.) "My mind feels like it's going a million miles an hour. And I really don't want to move to northern Virginia. It's not what I want to do."

"Well, if you would allow me to be frank with you—" (like he was really giving me an option) "—it sounds like God is trying to get a hold of your mind, brother." His voice had suddenly taken on an overtly spiritual tone. "And you're not letting him. Matthew, I've known you for a couple of years now—I don't know you very well, but I do know that you're a very passionate guy. I like the way you think; you think big and you think free. And I know you love God. But I think you are still holding on to control of your life. I don't believe you've relinquished your mind to God. Give him your mind, my friend, and you will be truly free."

"To be blunt, I've tried doing that, but nothing seems to work. I honestly don't know how to let him have my mind anymore. I've lost count of how many times I've taken it back from his hands."

My friend let out a big, robust laugh. "It's not brain surgery, Matthew. Just obey him. God changes our minds through our obedience to him. You know that!"

After much thought, debate, and frustration, I decided to obey God. Two months after talking to my pastor friend about my dilemma, I moved to northern Virginia.

{ **MY DEFINITION: dilemma**
Anything big or small standing in my way or challenging my way of thinking; anything that keeps me from getting my way. God is a big dilemma.

God takes hold of our minds through our obedience to him. It's counterintuitive, but we gain so much more when we let go to God. When we abandon our own ways of thinking and our own agendas and decidedly obey God's calling in our lives, we become much more aware of *his* agenda. In other words, we get to know—really know—what is important to him. We begin to realize what he values, what he hates, what's on his heart—and we can't know these kinds of things about God without obedience. In time, we begin to want what he wants for us.

Think about it: In our obedience to God, our love for him is put into action. We show him that we love him through our obedience. It's not something we have to do to receive his love; on the contrary, it's an outpouring of our love for him. An active love for God always begins with our faith to obey. When we are obedient to God, we are making a decision to wholeheartedly trust his agenda. We are saying to God that we trust him to know better than we do. And the beautiful thing is this: When we trust him, God always reveals more of himself to us.

Consider what Paul wrote in Ephesians 3:14-17: "When I think of the wisdom and scope of God's plan, I fall to my knees and pray to the Father, the Creator of everything in heaven and on earth. I pray that from his glorious, unlimited resources he will give you mighty inner strength through his Holy Spirit. And I pray that Christ will be more and more at home in your hearts as you trust in him. May your roots go down deep into the soil of God's marvelous love" (NLT).

As we get to know God's "marvelous love" through trusting him, through our obedience to him, and through our mental surrender, our thinking about our personal situations—whether they are good or bad—begins to change. It's impossible to follow God with all your heart without your mind being changed for the better.

Consider Paul's words in Colossians 2:6-8: "And now, just as you accepted Christ Jesus as your Lord, you must continue to live in obedience to him. Let your roots grow down into him and draw up nourishment from him, so you will grow in faith, strong and vigorous in the truth you were taught. Let your lives overflow with thanksgiving for all he has done. Don't let anyone lead you astray with empty philosophy and high-sounding nonsense that come from human thinking and from the evil powers of this world, and not from Christ" (NLT).

THE MIND GAMES GET PERSONAL

Drinking Beer

by Darren E. Thornberry

In the waning hours of a business trip to, of all places, Las Vegas, God put his white-hot finger on my drinking habit. As I write this piece, I've been alcohol free since that night two months ago.

Something just felt so wrong about drinking twelve or fifteen beers on a Saturday night and leading praise and worship six hours later. Compound that with the fact that I was raising four kids, who found it unusual wading through a sea of empty bottles before they could sit down and eat a bowl of cereal at the kitchen table. Frankly, I was unable to go without the suds. It was simply an old habit that eventually grew into a problem. That night in Las Vegas, I surrendered the drink. Now I'm trying not to put a grid on what it's supposed to look like tomorrow. Just taking it day by day. And now the battleground has shifted from the beer aisle to my mind.

Coming off the suds was harder than I expected it to be. I banked on a week or two of discomfort. I got that and more. Now, eight weeks in, just the thought of a frosty glass makes me angry with God, my wife, and anyone else in sight. And if I give the enemy some room, he's right there with a flood of ideas:

"Hey, there's no problem anymore. You'd be absolutely fine to have one drink."

"Heck, don't have a beer, have a glass of wine. God knows you want to stay submitted in this thing, right?"

"I mean, d-a-n-g, it is St. Patrick's Day! Why not have one Guinness? You can celebrate the fact that you're now out of the woods. . . ."

The outcome is all about what I believe. When I truly believed that I could not yield drinking to the Father, that's exactly what happened—I did not give it up. I knew it was an idol in my life, but I believed that I needed its comfort anyway.

Thank God that he shook that up, because I wasn't going to change. Now that I believe that God is the source of all comfort, I am able to live without drinking. Hey, it's still painful. Seems like my body literally aches for a drink sometimes. But those moments create poignant choices. If I stop and think for a few minutes about how good a drink would be, I become indignant and snippy as Satan heaps on feelings of selfishness, loss, and confusion. (My wife can always see the change as it occurs.) But if I choose to thank God for allowing me to depend on him for every good thing, I ride out the moment of weakness with my mind and heart at peace.

Drinking was a mountain in my life, yet it simply had to move when I took my thoughts captive and surrendered them to God. At first, I wanted control of the details. He could have the drinking in a broad, nebulous context, but I would map that out. Wrong. He made my mind; therefore, my enemy is out to steal and twist every reasonable thought that directs me to God in prayer. God help me, I want to know his heart more than I want my next beer. —*Darren E. Thornberry enjoys a career in publishing and creative writing, and makes a little music on the side. But his diaper-changing prowess is the stuff of legend. With his lovely wife, Rebecca, and four children, Darren works and plays in Montgomery, Alabama.*

Conversation with my therapist-slash-friend

"Bill, do you like green tea? I never have cared much for it."
"I like it. I went to Japan once and had green tea over there, and for some reason, I just acquired a taste for it."

"Acquired a taste for what? It doesn't have any flavor. It just looks like cloudy pee and tastes like bad hot water."

"Oh, then you've never had good green tea, Matthew. You've probably only tasted the green tea that Chinese buffets carry—that stuff is not the good kind."

"Hmm, you're probably right. You're always right about this kind of stuff—at least you make me think so."

About three years ago, I met Allison Pauls. As a twenty-three-year-old up-and-coming lobbyist in Washington, D.C., Allison had her dream job of working as an assistant for one of the leading lobbying firms in the capital's political district. Not only did she feel that God had called her to this job; she felt that her work was making a difference in the world. However, out of nowhere and much to her surprise, God asked her to leave her job in the political world and go to seminary to work toward becoming a Presbyterian minister. I spoke with Allison at length about her onetime dilemma.

"My mom and dad both thought seminary was a great idea," she told me when we got together one afternoon at TGI Friday's. "When God first put it on my heart to go to seminary, I said no. In fact, it was a coldhearted no. I didn't want to go to seminary; I just couldn't get my mind around the idea of being a pastor or preacher for the rest of my life. The mere thought of it sounded absurd. And besides, I really liked my job at the lobbying firm."

Taking a sip of my drink, I asked Allison how she was so certain it was God who was calling her to be a pastor. I found her answer quite interesting.

"I've almost always known when it was God trying to get my

attention. When he wants you to do something, he hits you in the heart, the mind, and the emotions—sometimes even in the backside. However, just because his voice is so distinctive and so alive, that doesn't mean it's always easy to just follow him without a little fight, without questioning his timing. At that time, I honestly thought that for once God was out of his mind."

Allison fought with God for eighteen months before deciding to go to seminary. During that time, she candidly and openly admitted, she felt utterly depressed.

"I was severely depressed. During those eighteen months of running from God, of not being open to his will in my life, I felt overwhelmed, consumed, and completely stubborn. When I was in direct disobedience to God's desire for my life, I think a spiritual emptiness came over me and masked itself as clinical depression. I went on medication and everything. But for me, it wasn't a chemical imbalance like it is for some. It was plain and simple disobedience throwing my mind out of whack.*

"I think that is what the Bible is actually talking about when it mentions some of the problems the men and women of God faced. Consider the lives of David, Moses, and Jonah—I believe they felt that same thing [a depression of sorts] when they disobeyed God."

One night, in the middle of a huge argument with her mom, Allison's will broke. It was a day she will forever remember as life changing.

"Mom and I were fighting with each other over something political." She laughed but quickly told me that at the time the situation was anything but funny. "I was so angry and emotional and pissed off that my mom looked at me with her huge, mysterious brown eyes and said, 'This has nothing to do with my feelings about

* AUTHOR'S NOTE: I do not want to suggest with this story that all depression and anxiety cases are caused by disobedience. That is not the case. This was only Allison's experience and should not be taken as a blanket statement.

the death penalty, Allison. This little eruption you're experiencing is about you running away from a very serious God-calling, and you know it.' I was shocked. I was angry. I was out of my mind."

Later that night, she said, she had a lengthy confession time with God. A "get-down-on-my-face session with God" is what she called it.

"That next semester I went to seminary. I gave in. I humbled myself and listened to God. And I was finally free."

confessions of a strange mind

jessica and i had the most spectacular wedding day. every minute detail of our ceremony was perfectly scripted to display our love publicly in front of god, family, and friends. surrounded by those we love the most, jessica and i promised our love to each other "for as long as we both shall live." after a four-hour reception that included champagne, dancing, and a sing-along of billy joel's "piano man," jessica and i ventured upstairs to our fancy hotel room with the rose-petal-covered king-size bed.

as we sat on the bed, preparing for our first night of sexual freedom, i began to cry.

it wasn't just a whimper; it was an all-out sob. jessica didn't know what to say. think about this: my wife is sitting there ready—really ready—to consummate our relationship, and her husband (me) is sitting there crying like a blubbering fool. i cried for thirty minutes.

the events of the day weighed on me. having all the people i love the most in the same room for five hours was overwhelming and very special. my head was having a hard time calculating it all—so instead of calculating, i broke down. it's not necessarily easy *for me to admit this in writing, but today my wife and i get a good laugh out of it.*

the mind is powerful that way. it sometimes can't receive and properly distribute a bunch of experiences all at once. when people die, get sick, move away, refuse to talk to you—a mind struggles to make sense of it all.

after my thirty-minute sob session, jessica and i prayed together. and then we got busy with consummating. . . .

When we obey God's words, God's calling, God's commands, we are taking a giant leap forward toward freethinking. Consider Jonah. He ran from God's call with all his might. God followed him into a boat and into the belly of a fish. Jonah finally came back to God and surrendered his will. His freedom came when he completely gave in to God's will and just followed.

Unfortunately, that kind of surrender is not popular today. Everywhere we turn in our contemporary, self-help-driven society, we are encouraged to think for ourselves, to pursue an open and free mind, to find freedom from within. In many colleges and universities, professors are encouraging their students to think for themselves and not let anyone or anything limit or define them. The irony is that, instead of letting their students truly think for themselves, these professors are actually trying to get them to think the way the professors think. They slant their teaching in hopes of swaying young minds in a particular political, social, or emotional direction. Likewise, television and other media purport to encourage us not to be confined by conservatism or liberalism but to think for ourselves, while at the same time slanting their coverage or their "entertainment" in such a way that they advance a particular cause or point of view. And media celebrities often use their cultural prominence to make statements meant to influence us. I could go on and on about this, but I'm sure you've recognized it, too.

The Bible recognizes that the question is not *whether* we'll be influenced but *by what or whom* we will be influenced. The Bible teaches us that our minds find freedom through total submission to the authority of God. I personally believe that we are unable to begin freethinking until we learn to surrender our thoughts and actions to his desires.

Some might call this type of thinking radical, and others might consider it to be legalistic (I don't; as I said before, I hate legalism of any kind), but I have found in my own life that submission to God's purpose is totally freeing. It is when I'm *not* obeying God's directions, when I'm *not* pursuing a life of obedient faith, that I find myself locked up and unable to truly live the passionate and free life that God intended.

passiveness

PASSIVENESS IS A MIND GAME THAT'S ABOUT LIVING IN THE BACK-
GROUND, AVOIDING THE DECISIONS AT THE FOREFRONT OF LIFE.
IT'S HARD BEING FULLY ENGAGED IN THE PROCESS OF LIVING. A PASSIVE
LIFE FEELS SO MUCH EASIER, BUT IT BASICALLY CONTRADICTS GOD'S
DESIRE THAT WE BE PEOPLE WHO ARE FULLY ALIVE. WHEN WE'RE NOT
FULLY ALIVE, WE'RE NOT THINKING FREE. AND VICE VERSA.

Nicole was a model I dated for five months. I met her at a coffeehouse one evening, and believe me, it was fascination (not love)
at first sight. She was beautiful. She was talented. She was beautiful. And she wanted to have dinner with me the following Friday
night. She seemed perfect for me. (Did I mention she was a
model?)

Well, she and I fell for each other quickly. (Big surprise there,
huh? It's not like I am known for my slow-going relationships.)
Once-a-week dates turned into three-or-four-nights-a-week
dates. By the second week, I had kissed her. And she had kissed me

back. When week five rolled around, I proclaimed my love, and she proclaimed her love for me. At this point, in my mind, our relationship couldn't have been much better. Our love affair was like a storybook romance, seamless and triumphant—at least, that's what I thought at the time.

Five months into our whirlwind relationship, Nicole and I had a moderate-size fight over something very small and meaningless; however, she ended up saying a few very hurtful things to me. I didn't know how to handle it, so instead of staying calm and working through it slowly, I freaked out, broke up with her, and left her cold.

When I look back, it's easy for me to see that I didn't love Nicole the way I thought I did. Oh, I believe I loved her with my heart and at least part of my soul, and I probably even loved her with my strength, but that is still an incomplete love. I realize now that I didn't love Nicole with my mind.

Journal Entry: AUGUST 26, 1999

My mind gets in the way of my ability to love. I've thought I understood love before, but now I'm pretty convinced I don't understand it or don't have the energy or the will to show it.

Let me explain what I'm talking about in my relationship with Nicole, starting with a verse that has always fascinated me: "You must love the Lord your God with all your heart, all your soul, all your mind, and all your strength" (Mark 12:30, NLT).

This has got to be one of the most powerful and commanding principles that Jesus ever communicated. Its words are poignant and all-encompassing, somewhat demanding, and to us humans, even a little greedy. But that's not why this verse fascinates me.

What caught my attention is that Jesus identifies four distinct parts to our humanity—we all have a heart, a soul, a body (strength), and a mind. This might seem simple enough to you, but it's what Jesus instructs us to do with these four parts that I find so intriguing. With a mere twenty-two words, Jesus calls us to gather together all four dependent fragments of the human experience for one life cause—to emphatically and completely love his Father.

I don't use the words *dependent* and *fragments* lightly. Think about this: Without each of the four parts working together as a complete unit, we are left with very little. I believe that Jesus was saying that unless we love God completely, with all four parts of our humanity, love does not truly exist. His words acknowledge a very common human weakness: We are prone to love with only part of our being. Because Jesus, as God, made us the way we are, he knows the inner workings of our humanity; he knows that these separate parts must also be congruent. He made his desire for us rather simple; he didn't mince words. He simply said, "I want your hearts, souls, bodies, *and* minds to be completely in love with the Lord your God."

God's desire, and his commandment, hasn't changed in two thousand years. Today, Jesus still calls his followers to a pure and undivided love for his Father. He wants us to jump in—or dive in, if you prefer—with everything we are. He wants us to invest all of ourselves into loving him.

When we love God like this—when all four parts of our being are harmonizing together—something miraculous happens. Not only is the love we show to God (and to others) made complete, but I believe *we* are made complete as well. Jesus knows this about us, and that's why he calls us so emphatically to this kind of love and commitment.

Dating and Love

by Dottie Hutcherson

I worked my way past the crowds that were bottlenecking at the entrance, and I scanned the room for his face. Every guy could have had his hair color and been wearing his jacket, but I could always pick him out in less than five seconds. My radar was programmed to zoom in only on him—all the other images were just blurs until my sights settled on his brown hair, his blue eyes, his nicely defined jawline, and . . . well, you get the picture. I don't know what it is that makes me this way, but I'm never interested in more than one guy at a time. And when I fall for someone—develop a schoolgirl crush like I'm fifteen instead of twenty-two—I fall hard. Usually, this involves putting my heart way before my head, like the proverbial cart before the horse.

On a rational, logical level, I understand that my crush and I are simply friends. Nothing more. Possibly something less. But despite this intellectual understanding, I still find myself caught up in a series of dangerous thoughts. I imagine what a date with him would be like: walking around downtown on a summer evening, watching a movie and snacking on homemade cookies, sitting in plastic chairs while rain falls on the balcony of his apartment. I call these mind wanderings dangerous because they have a way of breeding within me a sense of discontentment. The more frequently I allow myself to indulge in my romantic delusions, however harmless they may seem on the surface, the less satisfied I become with the current state of my life.

As my dissatisfaction increases, it becomes easier for me to doubt what it is that God has planned and purposed for my life. It's as if I know exactly what I want, but I don't see God working to bring those things (or people) into my life. This must mean he is asking me to wait and to trust that he is faithful. Elisabeth Elliot has said, "Waiting on God requires the willingness to bear uncertainty, to carry within oneself the unanswered question, lifting the heart to God about it whenever it intrudes upon one's thoughts." When I notice my thoughts drifting to some fabrication of what I wish my immediate future would be like, I need to take a moment to prayerfully consider the ramifications of my desires—desires that more readily seek instant gratification than patient faith. Each longing, each unfulfilled desire, is an opportunity to make a sacrifice to God, saying that I trust him to be faithful and that I am willing to face the momentary disappointment that comes from having my current cravings denied, because I have confidence that he is continuing to refine me and unfold his perfect plan in my life.

It's nice to have that funny feeling when I see that special someone—the feeling that I've just stuck my finger in an electric outlet, and I know I should remove it, but I just can't; I'm too caught up in the thrill of it all. And it's exciting and wonderful to have someone I can seek out in even the largest of crowds—a face that's simultaneously comforting and exhilarating. However, when these new thrills begin to preoccupy my thoughts and brew a dangerous restlessness in my soul, I know I need to sacrifice them at the feet of One who has promised to bring me a life more abundant than my temporary longings. —*Dottie Hutcherson recently completed a BA in English and writing at Indiana Wesleyan University and is working on her MA in English through the Indianapolis campus of Indiana University. When she's not daydreaming, she can usually be found reading something by Anne Lamott or Naomi Shihab Nye.*

I had this job right after college that became my first experience with a bad manager. Well, maybe he wasn't so bad, really, but there was something about him that made my personality shut down. As soon as he would open his mouth, I was affected by his tone and his lack of communication skills. His entire personality annoyed me. Over time, it became incredibly difficult for me to form a kind-spirited response to most of his questions or comments. I don't want to mislead you— this guy wasn't mean, really, but somehow his demeanor seemed pretentious to me. And truthfully, he was somewhat unintelligent about the kind of work we did.

However, instead of *trying* to like him or understand him or engage with him, I found it nearly impossible *not* to act indifferent toward him. Instead of knocking down the walls to build a relationship, my thoughts about him built a thick fortress around me. And I was convinced that this "fortress," which consisted primarily of my mental inability or unwillingness to get past my dislike for this guy, somehow protected me. Eventually, I became comfortable with my negative feelings, and sadly, I never got to a point where I felt otherwise.

It's so easy to become inert in our relationships. Whether it's prejudice, poor thinking, or just laziness, too often we choose to stay disengaged from people. We just don't deal with stuff. Passiveness can be a kind of drug.

In my relationship—or lack of relationship—with my boss, because I had deemed him weird, pretentious, and stupid in my mind, I turned him off and thereafter didn't try. My heart and emotions followed the condition of my mind.

How often do we do that with people?

confessions of a strange mind

when i was a teenager, i loved cutting the grass. my father had a good-size john deere riding lawn mower. every week i looked forward to getting on the lawn mower. i didn't look forward to it because i got to be outside or because i particularly liked being on a fast-moving object. no, i liked mowing the lawn because i got to talk to myself while on the mower. because the mower was so loud, i could talk to myself and no one would ever hear what i was saying, which was a very nice feature, i might add. i talked to myself about being an actor and a writer. i'd pretend i had just finished writing this well-loved book and oprah was now interviewing me. oprah's audience always loved me, of course. I was constantly a guest on that show. o and i became good friends because of it. anyway, every time i would cut the grass, I would imagine myself being somewhere other than where i was—in ninety-five-degree heat and humidity, cutting the grass.

I think the mind struggles to truly love. In fact, I believe it's harder for our minds to love than any of the other three parts. The reasons begin here: Our minds tend to be shallow, dirty, busy, and filled up. We jam them with hurtful information, painful circumstances, angry reactions, disgusting news, and bad thoughts. My own mind struggles to comprehend and decipher all the things that get put into my head.

More than likely, all of us process everything we see, feel, experience, hear, and know with our minds first. Before our hearts, souls, and bodies have a chance to respond, our minds have already grabbed the information and stored it away. Everything, and I mean everything, we put into our minds or experience with our minds becomes part of our long-term memory. Sometimes it becomes part of our character. Sometimes it simply becomes knowledge. But no matter how big or small, all the information we take in gets programmed inside our brains.

Take a moment and think about the last time you had to forgive someone. Your heart and soul probably tried to reach out in true forgiveness to the person who had done you wrong. You may have wrapped your arms around the person in an embrace—and perhaps the experience even caused you to fight back tears. Nevertheless, for the rest of your life, what that person did will always be lodged in your memory. Forgiveness, from the mind's point of view, takes extra work—it takes quite a few more steps. Sometimes, our minds are unwilling to simply "forgive and forget." We have to *choose* to forgive over and over and over again. Still, it's a practice we must learn to do and do faithfully.

Conversation with my therapist-slash-friend

"What's wrong with you, Matthew?" Bill asked abruptly during one of our little talks. I'll be honest; I was in a foul mood.

"Nothing is wrong with me," I responded just as abruptly.

"Why don't you just admit what's wrong or get over your little PMS session."

"I'm not PMSing!"

"Sure sounds like you're PMSing to me. And to be honest with you, it's quite unbecoming."

"What's that supposed to mean?"

"Let me give you some very good advice. Never act outside of what is normal for your personality. In other words, it's not natural for you to act like a pompous jerk, so don't act like one. Frankly, you're not that good at it anyway."

"Thanks a lot, Bill."

"So, are you ready to move on and talk about the rest of your problems?" Bill said.

"Yeah, I guess so. I'm not well, am I?"

"Umm, I don't want to answer that right at this moment."

Jesus expects us to take the necessary steps to love him and others with our minds. It, too, is something we have to do over and over again until it becomes a habit. It's not just a request; it's part of the greatest commandment we followers of Jesus have been given.

Think about what the apostle Peter wrote in 1 Peter 3:8: "Finally, all of you should be of one mind, full of sympathy toward each other, loving one another with tender hearts and humble minds" (NLT). The phrase "humble minds" stands out in this verse. Peter is saying that in order to love, our minds must take the road of humility. When you consider that often our love for God is reflected through our love for one another, this verse sheds a pretty bright light on the subject of loving with our minds. But it's not such an easy task.

It's simpler, and even more natural perhaps, to love with our hearts and souls than with our minds. Think about it: Our hearts and souls are supposed to be emotional, warm, and active in love. It's an innate part of our humanity to show affection with our hearts and souls.

The heart is often where we've been taught that love resides, and it's usually where we first begin to feel the effects of love. Love begins in the heart and seeps into the other parts of our being.

The soul is often thought of as the center of our being, our personal core. The soul is where all the deep things exist, live, and breathe. The soul is where we feel the pain of a family member's death. Most of our passions are developed in the soul. And when we invite Jesus to become a part of our lives, he seals our souls for eternity. The soul is the deepest part of us; it is eternal and lasting.

Although we easily mix up the actions of our hearts and souls, they often function hand in hand. They are two very separate entities, but it's hard for us to respond with one and not the other.

Like our hearts and souls, our bodies seem predisposed to show love. This is pretty much self-explanatory, I would think. We humans have very little trouble revealing our affection through the medium of touch. We hug. We kiss. We tickle. We have sex. We pat each other on the back. We constantly show our love in physical ways. It comes naturally.

{

MY DEFINITION: soul
The part of me that feels the pain of truth in almost every situation I face. When the Holy Spirit kicks me in the soul, it feels a little like I've been kicked in the groin.

I have found that loving with our minds is difficult but necessary in order for love to be complete. Love with one of the components absent is not love at all. When a person's heart, soul, mind, and strength are in harmony with each other, then and only then can perfect love exist. But because our minds calculate and remember all that we have ever experienced, our minds struggle to love.

Most of us probably feel a deep love for someone in our family. Whether it's your mother, father, brother, sister, grandparent, or child, your love for them is probably rooted firmly in your heart, soul, mind, and body. How can you tell that it's that kind of love? Because it's the kind of love you don't have to think about—it just is because it's built inside every part of your being. It's the kind of love that overcomes sad experiences. It's the kind of love that conquers all. Some people never experience this kind of love outside of the relationships they have at home. And some don't even have that, because they can't seem to love with their minds. And if we humans fail to love with our minds, I believe we never truly love.

The mind is where we first think about love, but it's often the last place where love actually becomes a response.

On Friday April 11, 2003, I fell in love with the woman who became my wife. For the first time ever, I remember thinking that I could love someone with all my heart. And truly, on that day, I experienced human love like never before in my life. But to my surprise and wonder, that feeling, that emotion, was only the beginning. Heartfelt love begins with butterflies and long glances, but as it progresses toward becoming a lasting, eternal love, it swells into an overwhelming emotion that the heart cannot hold in. It's hard to even begin to describe the feeling. And usually, when your heart overflows with love for another person, you truly believe that it would be impossible for you to love someone any more than the love you feel at that moment.

But as time went on, my love for Jessica grew bigger, stronger, and deeper. What began in my heart began to overflow into other parts of my being. I first began to feel it in my body. It doesn't take a degree in psychology to comprehend this. Suddenly, I wanted to be with Jessica more, touch her more, hold her more, protect her more, and kiss her (a lot) more.

But still, love didn't stop there. It began pouring out of my heart and into my soul. And the depths of my soul were touched like never before. I began feeling emotions I had never experienced. I would see Jessica and tears would roll down my face. I began to hurt when she was hurting. I got excited when she got excited. When her heart moved, mine moved, too.

But again, love did not stop there. It wasn't until my love for Jessica filled my heart, my body, and my soul that love for her began to reign in my mind. And only then did I fully comprehend what my love for this woman was capable of feeling, experiencing, hoping—and forgetting. The little things that once annoyed me didn't annoy me anymore, because love was touching my whole being. My respect for her grew, because love was touching my whole being. Purity was a natural response, because love was touching my whole being. I did not even begin to experience the fullness of love until it had permeated my entire being.

Journal Entry: AUGUST 26, 1999

My therapist told me today that I need to get my heart and mind on the same page—a "good page" he actually said. I'm not exactly sure what he means by this, but that is certainly my goal—a unified heart and mind.

A mindful kind of love is powerful because it is *conscious* and *intentional*. It *chooses* to love despite—and because of—everything we know to be true about the other person. That's the kind of love that

God feels for us and the kind of love he wants us to feel for him. It's the only kind of love that is truly complete.

It seems rather basic and natural to feel love for God in our hearts and souls. And it's relatively easy for us to reveal our love for God with our actions—our strength. But too often, it seems, we stop short of a full and complete love when we shut the doors of our minds. You see, loving God (and others) with our minds requires us to *think* differently, to humble ourselves, to let go of our opinions, thoughts, ideas, prejudices, and preconceived notions about God, other people, and life. Loving God (and others) with our minds means that we love *freely* and thus *completely*. When we love someone with our minds, we love him or her with the part of our being that we hold most dear. That's the kind of love that God desires from us—a complete love—from our entire being.

Are you loving others (and God) with your mind? Strange question, I know, but one I keep asking myself.

C H A P T E R   4

codependence

CODEPENDENCE IS A BEHAVIOR IN WHICH A PERSON LIVES FOR AND
THROUGH THE LIFE OF ANOTHER PERSON. SOUNDS STRANGE, BUT
A LOT OF US DO IT. SOMETIMES IT LOOKS LIKE "HELPING" OR "SELF-
SACRIFICE," BUT IT REALLY IS FAR LESS NOBLE THAN THAT. SOMEONE ONCE
SAID THAT CODEPENDENCE IS LIVING OUTSIDE OF YOUR OWN REALITY
AND IN THE REALITY OF SOMEONE ELSE. PERHAPS THE MOST DAMAGING
OF ALL THE MIND GAMES WE PLAY, CODEPENDENCE NOT ONLY KEEPS US
FROM OUR GOD-FILLED POTENTIAL, BUT IT INTERRUPTS OUR ABILITY TO
LIVE ANY LIFE AT ALL. DEPENDENT UPON ANYTHING BUT GOD, YOUR MIND
IS IMPRISONED AND ANYTHING BUT FREETHINKING.

Journal Entry: MARCH 3, 2002

> *Mom says I'm codependent. She's probably right. I hate
> when she's right. I know that I need to be free of all this.
> But I'm struggling to know how.*

When you've lived much of your life having to fight your own battle with codependence, you quickly learn how to recognize it in other people. The truth is that most of us are at least somewhat codependent on someone or something. It's human nature, I suppose. All of us probably engage in relationships that suffer because of unmet emotional needs stemming from our childhood, our brokenness, or some other event in our lives. These seemingly subtle and innocent addictions we have to people or things come in all shapes and sizes, and of course, in varying degrees of seriousness. Honestly, one person's codependence might be another person's normal (and somewhat healthy) way of life.

Many people don't even know what codependence looks like. They don't know that you can be codependent to family, to approval, to situations, to people's problems, to friends, to an emotional feeling, or to a church or a pastor. There are no real "medical" or "professional" rules that apply universally when trying to define or diagnose codependence.

Codependence is often hard to recognize in one's own life. It took me many years before I could actually see it in mine, and sadly, it took me many more years before I learned how to deal with my codependent nature.

My awakening was sudden, almost like a light switch being flicked on inside my head. I began to see my chronic emotional, physical, and spiritual dependence on other people's approval. Before that moment, I had never considered that, instead of being dependent on my personal relationship with Jesus, I could be detrimentally dependent on something or someone else. But I soon realized that because of an unmet emptiness inside me, my adult life had become a prime breeding ground for codependent behavior.

If you, like me, have come to recognize your own unhealthy alliances, I'm sure you know all too well that codependence will relentlessly steal away your joy, freedom, livelihood, pride, and spirit. And it's often hard for God to freely use an individual who is codependent.

Truthfully, without your core center focused on God's ideal for your life, you can't be truly freethinking.

> We are a world full of codependent people because we are a people who are unsatisfied with ourselves. AUTHOR UNKNOWN

Consider twenty-eight-year-old John Rant's personal battle with codependence:

"I was the kid in school who was constantly seeking the attention of others. I didn't care whose attention it was; I craved it all. You see, I didn't get much attention at home. My parents weren't bad, necessarily. They just didn't give us kids—there were six of us—the kind of attention that most children need. I compensated by looking for that attention elsewhere. Looking back, I can now see that I was constantly seeking the approval of my teachers, my pastors, my coaches—even my parents. And you know, I could never figure out how to make that happen. I never got the approval I was looking for."

During John's sophomore year in high school, a run-in with his Algebra 2 teacher changed his life—but not for the better. "I was acting up, as usual. I had the entire class laughing at me. There were boys and girls practically rolling on the floor they were laughing so hard. Gosh, I can't even remember what I was doing now, but I'll never forget my teacher's reaction when he came back into the classroom. He hollered my name so loud that the kids from the special education classroom all the way down at the other end of the hallway heard him. Mr. Jones was an old family friend, and he'd been teaching for more than twenty years at the private school I went to. I had never seen him so angry in all my life.

"He came storming over to my desk, and by that time I was scared out of my mind of what he was going to do. He grabbed me by my left earlobe and literally slammed my head down onto my desk. And then, with his full Texas accent, he yelled in my ear as loudly as he could:

"'YOU EVER ACT UP IN MY CLASSROOM AGAIN, MR. RANT, AND I'LL KILL YOU.'

"He actually used the word *kill*. You could have heard a pin drop in that classroom. One girl actually started crying. Mr. Jones pulled me over to the corner of the room and made me stand there for four hours. I ended up urinating in my pants because Mr. Jones wouldn't let me go to the bathroom. I'm not lying; that's the truth."

John said his high school days were never quite the same after that experience. "No one took my side except my parents—that's it. The school administration did nothing. The kids in the classroom didn't even back me up. So I physically and mentally shut down. I mean, I was already a very insecure kid. I couldn't play sports and I didn't get good grades, so needless to say I was not the most popular kid in school. Honestly, I believe with all my heart that the after-effects of that situation messed up my life. . . . I've never been the same since."

It wasn't until John left for a small college in Dallas that he finally opened up and began to trust people again, but that turned out to be one of the worst things he could have done. That's where his true battle with codependence began.

"I met a guy named Sam Colby during my third week at college; we became the best of friends practically overnight. We were the kind of friends that people envied. For me, it felt so good to finally have someone I could call my friend. I'd never had that before. Well, it had been a while, anyway. And truthfully, I hardly knew how to treat a friend. The act of trust is hard to get used to again."

John's friendship with Sam grew strong over those first few months. Hardly a day went by when the pair didn't see each other or hang out or do something together. Most of the other students thought they were either attached at the hip or secretly gay. Neither was true.

"About three or four months after Sam and I met—gosh, I remember this like it was yesterday—I called him one Friday night to see when we were going to hang out. And he was already out with some other friends. I felt this jealousy form in my gut. It just hit me out of nowhere. Sam hadn't even called me to ask if I wanted to go. I know this sounds ridiculous, but something inside of me snapped. I felt like I had been betrayed. It was almost as if every little bit of emotion I felt when my friends didn't stick up for me in high school came washing back over me."

John hung up the phone that night without telling Sam how he felt. He was embarrassed that he felt the way he did, so he just buried his feelings. The next day, he tried calling Sam again, but his friend's phone went right to voicemail.

"I flipped out emotionally. I called him four times right in a row. I don't know why, but I felt like he was probably mad at me— that he didn't want to talk to me because I had done something wrong to him. And if that were true, I needed to make it right. I wanted to make it right—not for Sam's sake—but for my own sanity. I'll bet you I called him at least seven times that day without him calling me back."

John's codependent behavior became more and more frequent. He says he was constantly thinking that Sam was avoiding his phone calls. When Sam would finally call, everything turned out to be normal—like nothing had ever happened. However, the relief that John felt never seemed to last—at least not in his mind.

"I became so paranoid. These weird situations just began to happen again and again. And the more it happened, the more consumed I became. When Sam decided not to go out with our friends on a Friday night, I would usually back out, too. He became everything that represented cool to me. And I did everything I could to ensure that nothing came between us."

Their friendship went on like this for almost a year. "Sooner or later, Sam began to really avoid me. Who could blame him? I was acting like a freak. But when he avoided me, it made me that much more codependent. And it was beginning to affect every aspect of my life—my job, my ability to do ministry at church, and my relationships with other people. I honestly felt like I could not function without Sam in my life. And yes, I know that all of this sounds ridiculous. But when you're emotionally codependent, it's hard to notice ridiculous.

"It got to the point where I couldn't make decisions without Sam's approval, without his okay, without his nod of agreement. When he didn't call me, I would panic. I'd call him to make sure things were okay. But those phone calls usually made me feel worse, not better. When Sam didn't want to hang out, I had no one to hang out with. When he was hanging out with other friends and I didn't get invited, it felt like rejection. Looking back, it's embarrassing to admit that I once was one of those annoying codependent friends people try to avoid, but I was."

John says now that he was oblivious to his behavior back then. "I knew I was acting weird, but I had no idea things were this weird. In my mind, it actually translated as Sam being a jerk toward me. It didn't compute in my head that it was *my* problem. I thought it was just Sam being weird, and I didn't understand why."

I asked John what finally opened his eyes to the codependence.

"It was my mom. She finally helped me see that it was my problem and not something to do with Sam. But even when she confronted me, I thought she was crazy. I kept insisting that I was not the one being strange or mean; I was certain it was Sam."

Even when John recognized and acknowledged his problem, at first he didn't know what to do about it.

"This was like an addiction. I honestly thought that my life would fall apart if all of a sudden Sam were no longer a part of it. When I couldn't stop this behavior on my own, my mother encouraged me to see a counselor."

Ultimately, the only way he was able to free himself from his codependence on Sam was to make a hard decision to physically move away and attend another college. "It was the hardest thing to do," he said, "but I had to do it for sanity's sake. I had to get as far away from the situation as I could. Sam and I still talk. Heck, we're probably better friends now than before. But the difference is I don't care what he's doing right now. I don't care about his opinions anymore. Before, I would be worried that he was mad at me, doing something fun without me, or hating me. It was pathetic. Now that I have recognized this behavior in my life, I can be free of it."

By meeting with a Christian counselor over the past couple of years, John has made huge strides toward being free of his codependence.

A very important part of my process of finding some balance in my life—of learning how to see myself and how I relate to others and life more clearly—was to get clear that everything in my process relates back to me and my growth

process. I had to get past my codependent belief
that I was doing something for you—or you were
doing something to me. ROBERT BURNEY, AUTHOR
OF *CODEPENDENCE: THE DANCE OF WOUNDED SOULS*

John Rant's story is an extreme case of how codependence can consume an individual. You might be thinking that you're not like John,
so you aren't codependent. And that might very well be true. However, don't be too quick to assume. Codependence is more often a
subtle occurrence in one's life and not an obvious happening. Not all
people who are codependent are as extreme as John, yet his story
clearly illustrates some of the dynamics of codependence.

It might be your nature to constantly please people; it might be
your nature to become too attached too quickly to individuals you
are dating. Codependence isn't always a flashing neon problem that
everyone in the world can see. In simple terms, it's *you not truthfully
being you* because of fear, insecurity, anxiety, guilt, or emptiness.
Whenever an individual or a situation keeps you from being you,
codependence might exist. Only you, God, and perhaps a really
good therapist will know for sure.

One thing's for certain: God wants your mind. If you're constantly consumed with someone or something other than God, he will
do what is necessary to remove that obstacle from your life. He will
not leave you in a hopeless situation. It's his desire to have all of you.

{ **MY DEFINITION:** survival
Anything that resembles healthy. At this time in my life, getting up in the
morning to a cup of Starbucks coffee is about as close to survival as I can
imagine. Well, actually, a blueberry scone would be nice, too.

For two years, I fought a personal codependence similar to the type that John Rant faced. During my years of bondage, I had so much insecurity and emotional emptiness welling up inside me that I would cling to other people's lives for survival. I felt that I needed their consent or authorization before moving forward. Heck, I didn't just feel like I needed it; I wanted their opinions and approval. I felt like I needed the investment of other people. I didn't believe I could survive emotionally or mentally without it. So, in an effort to secure my own feelings, I tried to manipulate every aspect I could of my friends' lives in order to best suit my own.

Most of my friends had no idea that I was struggling so much. They no doubt thought I was a little strange or over-the-top, or even dramatic and obsessive, but they didn't know that inside I was selfishly trying to maneuver their lives to fit inside my box. But that's exactly what I was doing. When you're codependent, you will do anything to make yourself feel better. When I was knee deep in codependence, I did my best to manipulate every situation I possibly could—to better my own situation. If things didn't seem like they were going to go my way, I would panic, become depressed, and think that my world was coming to an end.

I see now that the irony of my codependence was that in finding my good feeling in others' lives I was really just making everything all about me.

Make it your ambition to lead a quiet life, to mind your own business and to work with your hands, just as we told you, so that your daily life may win the respect of outsiders and so that you will not be dependent on anybody.
1 THESSALONIANS 4:11-12 (NIV)

The first step in breaking the cycle of codependence is to recognize the behavior. You have to emotionally step away from the situation and attempt to look at it from a bystander's viewpoint. You've got to see your true motives for what they are. But that was hard for me. When you're codependent, it's hard to get yourself free enough to think outside the boundaries of your personal needs. When I was at the greatest point in my struggle and had people telling me that I was codependent, I didn't believe them. In fact, I thought they were completely off track.

But now I can see that even my denial was an effort to bury the fear I had of having to make some hard decisions—decisions that may have included leaving the situation, losing a friend, or simply admitting I was codependent. At the time, I just couldn't see it.

Before I could break free, I had to get away and ask God for his eyes to see the true me. I needed to see my situation as he saw it. And one of the many things I have learned about God through all of this is that when you ask him to help you see your life as he sees it, he is always quick to respond.

Through much pain and frustration, God gave me a true picture of myself. He allowed me to see myself in a way that I never had before—as a completely dependent soul unable to truly live free because of my emptiness. When God sheds his light on a situation, you always get a picture of truth. And although truth is ugly at times, it's where freethinkers always begin. I will be the first to admit that codependence is one of the hardest issues I have ever battled in my life. But when God opened my eyes and I could see not only a picture of myself but also a picture of what he wanted me to be, I was certain that freedom—in freethinking—was the place I needed to get to.

Conversation with my therapist-slash-friend

"Bill, what's your best advice for a Christian young man who is struggling to keep his mind clean in an over-sexualized culture?"

"Is this young man you, Matthew?"

"It's a friend, Bill, a good friend of mine who is struggling."

"Well, I would probably tell your 'friend' to come and set up an appointment with me so I could learn more about the nature of this individual's struggle and then give him some advice."

"I hate you, Bill. You know very well the 'young man' is me. Why do you have to mess with my mind like this? Why can't you just give me the advice I'm looking for?"

"Matthew, the best advice I can ever give someone is to own their problem. When you own your struggle, you have taken the first step toward freedom."

So much of the codependence mind game derives from early life experiences we've had that undermine our sense of value and worth. They challenge our identity. In adult life, then, we seek our own identity through the identities and lives of others.

In my own struggle with identity and codependence, I've gotten a lot of help from the Bible. First Corinthians 12:25-27 says this: "The way God designed our bodies is a model for understanding our lives together as a church: every part dependent on every other part, the parts we mention and the parts we don't, the parts we see and the parts we don't. If one part hurts, every other part is involved in the hurt, and in the healing. If one part flourishes, every other part enters into the exuberance. You are Christ's body—that's who you are! You must never forget this. Only as you accept your part of that body does your 'part' mean anything" ("The Message").

I've learned that knowing your place in the body of Christ gives you meaning. No longer are you simply the kid who got beat up in high school or the young woman with a horrendous sexual past or the college student with the displaced feelings. You are now part of a living body that needs your participation. There is freedom in knowing your place in God's world.

Codependence is usually built on untrue thinking. In order to be free from most mental illnesses, but especially codependence, you have to base your thoughts on truth. It's sometimes difficult for a codependent soul to see truth. Don't rely on your own thoughts; only God's Word can deliver the truth you can build your life on. "Jesus said to the people who believed in him, 'You are truly my disciples if you keep obeying my teachings. And you will know the truth, and the truth will set you free'" (John 8:31-32, NLT).

When you know your foundation, when you can fathom truth, hold on to it with all the passion and gusto you can muster. Your foundation in God's truth must be the place you call home, the place where you live. Isaiah 28:15-16 says, "You boast, 'We have entered into a covenant with death, with the grave we have made an agreement. When an overwhelming scourge sweeps by, it cannot touch us, for we have made a lie our refuge and falsehood our hiding place.' So this is what the Sovereign LORD says: 'See, I lay a stone in Zion, a tested stone, a precious cornerstone for a sure foundation; the one who trusts will never be dismayed'" (NIV).

These words from the Bible are one of the ways God has helped me in my struggle. Maybe they can help you, too.

lies

RELYING ON LIES IS LIKE A GUY PLAYING SOCCER WITHOUT WEARING A CUP. SURE, YOU MIGHT GET BY FOR A TIME BUILDING YOUR LIFE ON UNTRUTHS, BUT WHEN YOU EVENTUALLY LOSE THIS MIND GAME—AND YOU WILL—IT HURTS LIKE NO OTHER PAIN IMAGINABLE. LIES CRIPPLE YOUR ABILITY TO THINK WITH THE FREEDOM THAT GOD DESIRES. ONCE YOU EXPERIENCE THE DEVASTATION OF LIES, YOU EITHER BEGIN TO CAPTURE THE POWER OF TRUTH OR YOU START THE GAME ALL OVER AGAIN. IT'S AN UGLY CYCLE.

When Georgia native Cheryl Simons was a child, she always thought of herself as ugly. If you had talked to her when she was fifteen, she would have been able to quickly rattle off a long list of things she didn't like about herself. She never liked the texture or color of her hair. She hated her large hips and flabby stomach. She thought her nose was monstrous and her lips too thin. And her teeth—she thought her teeth were atrocious. Cheryl liked very little about her appearance. It started when she was in middle school.

From the time she was eleven years old, stumbling through the awkward phase of puberty, she would look in the mirror and tell herself she was ugly, fat, and not worthy of boys' attention.

Sadly, her thought life was destructive because she believed every word. She told herself that she would never marry because she wasn't as pretty as some of the girls she knew. She believed it. She told herself she wouldn't be as successful as other girls because of her weight. She believed that, too. She told herself that people looked down on her because of her teeth. By the time she was sixteen, Cheryl had thoroughly convinced herself that her life really wasn't worth living, mostly because of her appearance. She not only believed all the things she had told herself, but she began to live as if the lies she had told herself were truth.

As she got older, her demeanor worsened. Not only did she feel ugly, but she was also very depressed, perhaps a little suicidal, and felt very much alone.

Cheryl's mother realized that something was emotionally wrong with her daughter, so she took her to see a counselor a week before Cheryl turned seventeen. The counselor listened to the young girl's tearful story as Cheryl told her everything. From her demeaning thoughts to her insecurities about her body, she laid every powerful thought out on the table for the counselor to see, hear, and feel.

As soon as Cheryl finished her story, the counselor looked at her and said with a smile, "I've got some good news for you. Today's the first day of freedom for you. Have you ever felt freedom before? Today's the day you're going to stop basing your entire life around lies and begin building a new life on truth. I'm going to help you do just that."

Although Cheryl hardly believed the words when the counselor made her look into a mirror and say, "I am pretty," the thought did make her smile a bit—just not with her teeth showing. It took more than two years for Cheryl to get to a place where she could stop believing the lies she had built her world on for more than six years. For six years, Cheryl had belittled herself, put herself down, and fed her mind destructive thoughts and words that she firmly believed to be true. Today, at age twenty-four, Cheryl has recently graduated from college with a degree in physical therapy and is planning to attend graduate school. She's dating someone seriously, but no wedding date has been set.

As Cheryl Simons discovered, the lies and falsehoods she continually told herself became a cage in which she lived. They became her reality. She found out the hard way something that we all must understand: Our minds hold a great deal of power over our lives. Whatever we feed our minds, whatever lies or truth we consume, will eventually begin to define not only how we think but also who we are as people. We cannot survive for very long in a cage of lies. Lies may give us a temporary illusion of life, but eventually they suck the breath right out of us. When we build our world on lies, when we believe untruths, we end up living fragmented lives. Fragmented lives are not what God intended for his children.

Journal Entry: APRIL 3, 2001

> *I read the book* Telling Yourself the Truth *today. I never realized how much I lie to myself. It's incredible what my mind is willing to believe.*

Even though I believe myself to be a pretty self-aware person, I often fail to see the lies I tell myself. It's easy to underestimate self-deception. When our foundation is pride or fear or independence, it's often easier to believe what we tell ourselves than what God or other people tell us. Telling ourselves lies can wreak havoc on the way we think and the way we live. On the other hand, telling ourselves the truth can also be powerful and life changing, but in the right direction.

I can't tell you how many times I have led myself into believing my own lies. At times in my life, I've thoroughly convinced myself that I'm ugly, worthless, incapable, fat, hopeless, perfect, or almighty.

I've realized that I need to speak truth to myself, or I can easily be convinced of almost anything. The truth of Jesus is the only element that can keep my mind—and yours—clean of self-deception.

{ **MY DEFINITION:** self-deception
Anything stupid, selfish, immature, codependent, lustful, agnostic, or mean-spirited that I believe to be 100 percent pure and true. Basically, any thought I have absent of God's influential grace.

Shane is one of those guys whose talent makes me sick. He plays six instruments, has a raspy falsetto for a singing voice, and writes soulful songs that move people to get up and shake their bodies. When I met this gutsy performer, it was obvious that he had more talent in his pinky than most people have in their entire bodies. And since the time that we first met, it's quite possible that the time Shane has spent on the road playing in clubs around the region has made him an even better musician and songwriter.

I met Shane in 1998 when he led praise and worship at a young-adult Bible study. His nontraditional approach to worshipping Jesus was refreshing. It was a raw musical worship that still gives me chills when I think about it. I looked forward to seeing where God would eventually take this young man. I was sure he would be used in some powerful way.

But time and circumstance eventually altered Shane's view of Jesus. Instead of running toward the Cross, he ran in the opposite direction. His desire to admit his own need for Jesus began to evaporate. He walked away from Christian things and decided to ask his big questions outside the walls of the church. He's still asking those questions.

He began singing lead vocals for a rock band that traveled around the mid-Atlantic region. That led to a lifestyle change that he exhibits quite regularly today. Honestly, I don't care that Shane gets drunk most evenings, smokes pot, and has sex with his girlfriend. I am much more concerned for his spirit. That kind, gentle, Jesus-like spirit has faded. "I don't *not* believe in Jesus," he told me a few years ago. "I don't know, Matt, I just feel different toward him. I'm not sure he really cares what I do. He needs to be busy saving the world, anyway; it's going to hell in a handbasket. You think I'm going to hell, huh? I actually don't care what you think; I'm having too much fun where I am."

When my buddy said those words, I couldn't help but wonder what lies he had convinced himself to believe. Were they his own thoughts? Was he telling himself the *un*truth?

Today, Shane remains in the trenches somewhere between truth and lies, which is a really dangerous place to be. The lies are much more believable in the middle.

Conversation with my therapist-slash-friend

"Matthew, you ever hear of the singer Eva Cassidy?"

"Nope, who is she?"

"Oh, she's this marvelous singer who didn't become famous until after she died of breast cancer."

"That's sad—I hope if I am destined to be famous, I become famous before I die."

"I don't know. It sounds like it would be a lot easier to be famous after you die."

"What do you mean?"

"Think about it. If you become well-known after you die, you still get to leave a lasting impact on the world, yet you never have to fight the pride, lust, and emptiness that often comes with fame."

"I guess that's true . . . but isn't the joy that comes with fame worth the battle with pride, lust, and emptiness?"

"You're missing the entire point, Matthew. It's pretty obvious you should never be famous."

"I'm a coffeehouse manager; I don't think I'll ever have the opportunity to become famous."

"Yeah, that's for sure."

"I don't know whether I should laugh or cry about that."

"I think you should cry; crying is humbling."

It's hard to accept the truth of what we are—people who may never become famous, don't have Shane's talent, or aren't as attractive as someone else. Sometimes these things are perfectly obvious to everyone but us. We find ways of spinning the facts and distorting the truth to help us feel better about ourselves.

We become prone to telling ourselves these untruths so we can "be" the person we want others to think we are. Some of us have lied to ourselves so often that we really don't know anymore what it means to think the truth. Truth has become foreign to us. Our reality has been altered. We've become distanced from our true selves, and we've lost the very thing that made us real and authentic and true.

Getting out of that place and getting into the right place—where we are building our lives on God's truth—is a difficult task.

If you've been building your life on lies, you know that getting to a place where truth reigns supreme in your mind is probably one of the greatest challenges you will ever face. But it's a fight worth every scar and every battle wound. Honestly, it wasn't until I began to allow my entire thought process to be filtered through the lens of God's truth that I believe I truly started living. When our minds are filled with untruths and half-truths, we're merely existing, and we're not truly living the life that God intended. The goal of freethinking is to get us back on track.

If you're like me, at one time or another you've survived on little white lies. Heck, maybe you've even used huge lies as temporary life support just to keep yourself moving in a particular direction. But lies don't last. Lies suffocate us, and they lead us toward depression, dissatisfaction, and anxiety. Believing lies to be truth only leads us to believe more lies. It becomes a web of deceit.

Like most people, I have had seasons in my life when truth was hardly my focus. In fact, I've had seasons when I lied to myself so much that my whole life was practically a lie. These seasons were exhausting. It wasn't that I necessarily turned my back on God; I just didn't have my mind fixed on him and what he stands for. It was during these periods of life that I fell hook, line, and sinker for my own brand of truth. It's the kind of truth I call human truth. Human truth might be something simple, such as being told "You look beautiful today." This might very well be true, but it's not truth you can build your life on. It's not the kind of truth that Jesus cares about. Unfortunately, when we take this kind of truth and make it bigger and more important than it's supposed to be, we have problems.

You see, human truth is subjective. It disguises itself as objective or transcendent truth, but it's really not objective truth at all. It might be factually true, but it's not the kind of truth we should be building our lives on. Human truth often comes in the form of statistics and facts. We might, for example, hear that 90 percent of the world's people believe in God, but because God's word contradicts that "human truth," we can't depend on it. Human truths are often statements built around what society believes to be true, and random theories by philosophers, professors, and pundits. Usually, human truth has just enough real truth built into it to attract a following. But when this human truth scrapes against God's truth, it's still a lie, no matter how minute the falsehood. But people are creating and buying into these "truths" all day long.

{

MY DEFINITION: attributes of truth

Truth never contradicts God's word.
Truth will not leave you empty, depressed, or anxious, unless you're still not convinced.
Truth is never irrational or unorganized.
Truth is willing to kick you in the butt if necessary, is usually not the popular way to go, and will not say, "Excuse me" before entering a situation.
Truth always eventually brings clarity of mind.

I can't remember exactly when I fell in love with the concept of objective truth—God's truth—and began to understand the power it can wield in my life. I just woke up to my self-deception and the lies that I had made myself believe.

Over the past couple of years, I have managed to fall head-over-heels in love with what truth means to my daily existence and my overall quality of life. Sure, the whole truth thing might sound like a simple concept, or perhaps it seems pretty obvious, but the long-term effects of this love affair with truth on my mind have been remarkable.

Consider how Eugene Peterson translates John 3:20-21 in *The Message*: "Everyone who makes a practice of doing evil, addicted to denial and illusion, hates God-light and won't come near it, fearing a painful exposure. But anyone working and living in truth and reality welcomes God-light so the work can be seen for the God-work it is." When our minds are consumed with lies, we become fearful of what Peterson calls "God-light." The light of God reveals truth. Jesus says that those who work and live in truth will welcome the light. They won't fear the light because their deeds are built on truth.

I firmly believe that if we anchor our minds to God's real, un-adulterated truth, the result will be a miraculous freedom that will completely alter our way of thinking. It will bring us into a state of freethinking. Truth ignites our realities because it gives us a base on which our thoughts can depend. When our minds are set on truth, we have a sturdy foundation that no one can touch, no storm can knock down, and no tornado can destroy. Only God's truth is that kind of foundation.

The only kind of truth that leads to freethinking is God-focused truth. Not "human truth." No other truth will satisfy our soul's need to think freely. No other truth will release us from our emotional, codependent, and spiritual chains. When Jesus said that the truth would set us free (John 8:32), what kind of truth was he talking about? We've heard everyone from Oprah to the Dalai Lama quote this verse. Presidents have quoted this verse. Atheists and agnostics, Christians and Muslims, professors and simpletons have quoted this verse. But more often than not, they've quoted it out of context. They aren't speaking of the same kind of truth that Jesus was. He did not say that *any* truth would set us free; he was referring to the truth about himself—who he is and what he was about to do—that would set us free. In John 8:31, the verse right before the "truth will set you free" verse, it says, "Jesus said to the people who believed in him, 'You are truly my disciples if you keep obeying my teachings'" (NLT).

Ouch! That verse bites a little if you're not a Jesus follower. Here, Jesus is talking about true belief and encouraging his followers to continue obeying his teachings. That's the context in which he said the truth would set us free. His words about truth leading to freedom are almost an afterthought to his remarks about our obedience to his teachings.

It would be easy for me to suggest that Cheryl Simons, the girl who was so unhappy with her life that she wove a fabric of lies to create a different identity for herself, was missing the truth that she was indeed beautiful and slender, with a beautiful smile and perfect teeth. But that isn't true, and it has nothing to do with God's truth, anyway. Cheryl *was* a little heavier than others in her class. Cheryl *wasn't* quite as pretty (by our society's standard of beauty) as some of her friends. But those truths are not what she needed to build her foundation on. The objective truth—God's truth— is that Cheryl is valuable to God (he created her!) and thus she is infinitely worthy. Her place in the Kingdom of God is not based on superficial qualifications. God looks at the heart, not the skin.

Cheryl's value to God is a truth she could build her life around. It's the kind of truth that all of us can build our faith on.

For a long time, Cheryl's memories and old ways of thinking often pushed her back into believing human truth—that looks matter, that she was just an ugly girl with crooked teeth, that marriage was out of the question because she was homely. Every time she believed the lies her mind was telling her, she easily slipped back into old patterns of depression, discouragement, and anger.

But as she pursued healing in her life, she began mustering up the strength and resolve to say, "No, depression! I'm not going with you. I'm choosing not to believe in you today. Instead, I'm putting my trust in what I know to be God's truth. I'm going to build my foundations on what he says to be true and not the lies you speak."

Cheryl's decisions to not believe the lies her mind was telling her became building blocks in a growing foundation of living based on objective, God-centered truth. Each act of the will, each refusal to give in was a beginning step in the right direction. Some people are surprised to discover that that's all God requires of us. He simply wants us to believe in him, to take a chance and choose to trust his dreams and passions and vision for us instead of falling for the world's untruths. Can you take a chance? Are you willing to let your mind sell out to God's truth?

> But God's truth stands firm like a foundation stone with this inscription: "The Lord knows those who are his," and "Those who claim they belong to the Lord must turn away from all wickedness." In a wealthy home some utensils are made of gold and silver, and some are made of wood and clay. The expensive utensils are used for special occasions, and the cheap ones are for everyday use. If you keep yourself pure, you will be a utensil God can use for his purpose. Your life will be clean, and you will be ready for the Master to use you for every good work. 2 TIMOTHY 2:19-21, NLT

It has only been in the past few years that I have begun to comprehend the power and complexities of the mind. As the body's computer, the mind saves, calculates, and analyzes everything we experience in life. The mind computes both positive and negative thoughts. Those thoughts often war against one another in an effort to control our heart, mind, and soul.

Several years ago the Academy Award–winning movie *A Beautiful Mind* gave many of us a new perspective on how fragile the human brain can be. As I watched John Forbes Nash (portrayed by Russell Crowe) endure an extreme mental battle between what was true and false in his experience, I couldn't help but see aspects of my own mental and spiritual battles. I think we all could learn a lesson from *A Beautiful Mind*. We learn that it's often very difficult to leave harmful thinking behind—even when we know it's harmful thinking—and to rest instead in the truthful hands of God.

The Bible is certainly not silent on the topic of the mind. It gives us clear guidelines. For example, 1 Chronicles 28:9 says, "Serve [God] with wholehearted devotion and with a willing mind, for the Lord searches every heart and understands every motive behind the thoughts" (NIV). God also gives advice to those who find truth and lies warring against each other in their minds. Isaiah 26:3 says, "You [God] will keep in perfect peace him whose mind is steadfast, because he trusts in you" (NIV). That peace is built on trusting in God, on trusting in his truth. Romans 12:2 urges followers of Jesus to be "transformed by the renewing of your mind" (NIV). This verse is a good reminder of how we must continually return to God and ask him to give us new passion, new grace, and new thoughts. All of these verses are powerful and influential reminders of what our minds need, but they also speak to how our relationship with Christ weighs heavily in navigating our thoughts toward perfect peace and toward knowing what God's truth is.

We will continue to struggle sometimes with the concept of God's truth. Like you, I want to experience truth to the fullest. But it's challenging sometimes not to be worried, anxious, or doubtful. At times, our minds will still try to deliver lies or human truths.

We'll be tempted to worry or to act in codependent ways or to attach our lives once again to fleeting human truths, as if that is the only way to survive. But each and every time that happens, we must come back around and realign ourselves with God's objective truth—about himself, about us, and about the world in which we live.

Four things that King David did with truth:

- He meditated on it. "I will walk in freedom, for I have devoted myself to your commandments. I will speak to kings about your decrees, and I will not be ashamed. How I delight in your commands! How I love them! I honor and love your commands. I meditate on your principles" (Psalm 119:45-48, NLT).

- He proclaimed it. "Truth springs up from the earth, and righteousness smiles down from heaven" (Psalm 85:11, NLT).

- He desired it. "Teach me your ways, O LORD, that I may live according to your truth! Grant me purity of heart, that I may honor you" (Psalm 86:11, NLT).

- He learned to follow. "Send out your light and your truth; let them guide me. Let them lead me to your holy mountain, to the place where you live" (Psalm 43:3, NLT).

Throughout my life, God has been faithful about bringing me gentle reminders from people I know and love who point me back to the truth. I vividly remember a conversation I had with one of my best friends, who shared his heart with me. He told me he thought I was a victim of fear and that my resistance to truth was due to the fact that I was not fully grasping the idea of being God's child. My mother has also constantly and avidly reminded me that God's truth comes in due time, that we must be patient, but never cease to search for it. I believe that God puts these kinds of reminders in all our paths, but our minds must be open to the possibilities.

One of my first victories on the road to recovering my mind and learning how to think free was realizing that truth isn't something I merely feel; it's something I have to actively pursue. Truth isn't always staring me down; it's more often a journey I must take. Sometimes I have to work at uncovering truth. Sometimes I have to change the way I think or alter my behavior before I can comprehend truth. What it all comes down to, I believe, is that every day I have to get to a place in my mind where I am trusting that God's truth will be revealed. And regardless of what my mind is telling me, I must believe in God's truth with all my heart, mind, soul, and strength. John Nash's problems didn't go away, but he learned to respond differently to the lies his mind was telling him—that's what changed. He learned how to grab on to what was true and to say no to what was untrue. If we want to think free, we have to get to the same place. We have to get to a place where we anchor our minds on truth.

Freethinking can't exist without truth.

distraction

EACH DAY YOU'RE DISTRACTED BY A MILLION THOUGHTS. YOU CAN
HANDLE IT ALL PRETTY WELL, YOU THINK, BUT AT A CERTAIN POINT,
YOUR MIND IS FLITTING FROM ONE THOUGHT TO ANOTHER TO ANOTHER
SO FAST THAT YOU CAN'T FOCUS ON ANY ONE THING. IT'S THE NATURE
OF MODERN LIFE. THE MIND GAME IS IN HOW WE DEAL WITH IT. IN A
SENSE, WE'RE ALL ADHD.

When I was ten years old and in the fifth grade, I spent more time staring at the brown-and-tan polka-dotted carpet than I did looking at my teacher. For some reason, I liked staring at the carpet. Usually when I did, the dots would come to life right before my eyes. My imagination took those ordinary dots and created shapes, words, and pictures right there on the floor. Sooner or later, my pretty little sightings would be chased away by a loud noise.

"MATTHEW TURNER!" My forty-something male teacher, a miserable excuse for a human being, would be addressing me in full decibel from the front of the room. "Can you please explain to me and the rest of the class why you're staring at the rug?"

Most of the class would laugh. Some kids would point at me and make comments.

"WELL?!" my teacher would say. "WE'RE ALL WAITING."

I often wonder what would have happened if I had told him the truth. What would he have done if I had told him that I was staring at the brown-and-tan-polka-dotted carpet and my mind was making those brown dots dance? What if I had said, "And, Mr. Calhoun, when the dots dance, I see things that no one else can see. I see shapes and letters and words. It's quite fascinating!"

But I never told the old geezer the truth. I always looked at him and said, "Nothing, sir."

"YOU MOST CERTAINLY *WERE* DOING SOMETHING!" he'd yell in response. Then he'd go back to teaching about adverbs and adjectives and pronouns and act as if my staring at the floor had interrupted the entire class. His words made me feel guilty and worthless. I just knew that he would tell my mom and dad, and more often than not he did.

Frankly, I didn't know why I stared at the floor. Believe me, if I could have gotten to the bottom of why I enjoyed staring at the carpet, I would have stopped doing it. I would have stopped doing a lot of things back then. But I know one thing: My undiagnosed childhood ADHD limited my ability on a lot of things. It kept my mind full and busy. It made my thoughts race quickly from topic to conversation to fear. It stole my ability to study; it made life in school difficult and awkward and boring.

When I was in my late twenties, I was officially diagnosed with adult ADHD. But before that, I had fought through the symptoms with determination, prayer and meditation, and a lot of confusion. It wasn't until I was the editor for *CCM* magazine that I realized I might need to seek some professional help.

Conversation with my therapist-slash-friend

"Bill, here's a question for you: Do you ever find that your mind just wanders from topic to topic to topic without rhyme or reason?"

"Umm, yeah, I think all of us have moments like that."

"Well, I don't necessarily just have moments when I'm doing that; it happens most of the time."

"Matthew, have you ever been diagnosed with ADHD?"

"No, I went to school before doctors were really in the mode of recognizing ADHD."

"Well, I think you probably have adult ADHD. Have you seen the new commercials for medications that treat adult ADHD?"

"You mean the one that shows several different middle-aged people wandering through their days, not sure what to do next, having a tough time concentrating?"

"Yeah, that one; I believe that's you."

"So, you think I have adult ADHD?"

"Yeah, I do."

"What's that mean exactly?"

"You now have a really good excuse for every stupid thing you do—and honestly, it's a great conversation starter."

"You always have such encouraging words for me."

"Hey, I do my best. And remember, my time with you is free. Just imagine what I can do when someone is paying me a hundred dollars an hour. . . . I'm a freakin' genius."

I have to confess to you that at times ADHD has been less a disease and more like a punch line to a joke I've often told. It's a quick way to get a few laughs when I am in front of large groups of people. It's an easy way to excuse my inability to listen and to hear, and a great way to remove myself from an awkward situation. ADHD has at times become a crutch. And when it does, it's a mind game that I play.

I've learned that I'm not the only one, and it's not just about ADHD.

The experts say that ADHD is one of several attention disorders. Some claim that attention disorders are not symptoms of a disease, but really symptoms of modern life. In some ways it's a response, even an addiction, to the pace and speed of daily life.

And in this sense, we're all affected. We're all wandering through life, struggling to focus, not sure which of dozens of things to do next.

And most of us play this same mind game—allowing the pace of our lives to populate our minds with busy, distracting thoughts and giving us excuses for our inability to focus on what really matters. We're distracted from those who mean the most—our families, ourselves, and God.

{ **MY DEFINITION: concentration**
A cruel tactic forced on me by school, work, relationships, and God, that often feels more like a punishment than a free state of mind.

One day, during the time when I was the editor of *CCM* magazine, one of my managing editors walked into my office. As soon as she stepped through the door, I knew she wanted to tell me something. She sat down in the chair in front of my desk and looked at me intently.

"I've been doing some research, Matthew," she said with a grin on her face. "And I believe you have 'adult ADD.' In fact, I think you have every symptom."

Her words took me by surprise. I didn't know how to respond. I was speechless. I wasn't sure if I was supposed to say thank you or tell her to get out of my office.

"Matthew, I have a friend who began taking medication for his ADD, and he is so much better off now. You struggle with concentrating, and I think this might really help you get more work done."

"Really?" I said, staring blankly at her.

"You're not offended, are you?" she asked.

"Oh gosh, no. Do I look offended?"

"A little."

"Well, it's just a little embarrassing to get diagnosed by someone at work. I mean, what if I came into your office and told you that 'I have been doing some research and it seems to me you have a clear case of narcissism.'"

"Oh, I can see where this might be similar to that."

"I know you didn't mean any harm by it; it's all good. I'm sure I'll be fine."

After my colleague left my office, I put my head down on my desk and cried.

"People are beginning to recognize something in my life, God, something I'm not sure how to handle," I said softly. "What am I supposed to do? How am I supposed to function when my mind is chock full of busyness and anxiety? Is there a remedy? If so, can you let me in on it?"

Journal Entry: JULY 14, 1998

My pastor told me to spend time each day meditating. So far, the only thing I've learned from it is that I have a big problem remaining still for more than three minutes.

Five years ago, I began practicing a form of meditation in my Christian walk.

No, I didn't start making a habit of sitting like a pretzel in the middle of my living room floor murmuring long monotone "ohms." And no, I'm not some yoga or Pilates extraordinaire. Honestly, when I first began meditating, it pretty much happened by accident.

Meditation began for me out of my desire to have a more informal and passionate and personal experience with Jesus. I had often asked God to reveal more of himself to me. I wanted to know him, but I couldn't get past my simple prayer life and my devotional-a-day books. Not that there's anything wrong with quiet times that include short prayers and devotionals; I just wanted more. I wanted to know God in a real way, and I made that request known to him often. He answered my yearning.

One night (it was mid-September) I wasn't able to sleep. So I got out of my bed to fetch some warm water and a saltine cracker. When I got back to my room that Tuesday morning at 2:37, I had an overwhelming feeling that God wanted my attention. I'll be the first to admit that I can't always explain that feeling. But when you experience it, you never forget it.

When it happened, almost instinctively, I sprawled facedown on the floor and simply remained still and waited on the Lord. In complete solitude, I listened for his voice again. I knew what I had heard, and I wanted to hear it again. I didn't know what God wanted, but I knew he had gotten my attention for a reason. After about twelve or thirteen minutes, I opened my Bible and began to read several different passages from the books of Job and Psalms. Eventually, my eyes fell on Psalm 19:14: "Let the words of my mouth, and the meditation of my heart, be acceptable in thy sight, O LORD, my strength, and my redeemer" (KJV). I read those words over and over again.

Right in the middle of my reading, I felt God nudge my heart with another request. *"Meditate on me and my words tonight."*

What? I didn't know how to meditate. I had never even tried it before.

"I'm not trying to be hard to deal with, God, but this is kind of awkward," I said out loud. "I know how to pray and read Scripture, but I don't know how to meditate." Again, as clear and crisp as the morning's black sky, I heard God speak again: *"Meditate on me and my words."*

I murmured back to him, "I will do my best to meditate on you."

Somewhat haphazardly, and not knowing what I was doing, I began to reflect on who God said he was, who he wanted to be in my life, how he had changed my life, and how he desired to be more integrated into what I did with my life. I contemplated God's Son, Jesus. I thought about the blood that Jesus shed on the cross. I thought about his unblemished life that he chose to sacrifice for me. I set my mind on the power of his resurrection and why his conquering of death meant I would be able to live forever. I thought about all of those things and more, but mostly I was quiet, still, and listening.

I stayed on the floor for more than an hour, hearing God, listening for his quiet voice, and experiencing his presence. I knew that I was not simply praying or reading Scripture or having a quiet time; I was communing with the God of the universe. I was having one-on-one time with the King of kings. This was no ordinary encounter. It was an experience like nothing I had ever felt before. I was meditating on my Savior, and through that time of meditation, he became more real to me.

After that experience, I felt a clarity of heart, soul, and mind that I had not experienced before. It wasn't simply "spiritual goose bumps" like one gets when hearing a God-powered story. My heart was clean. My soul was refreshed. My mind was renewed.

If our minds are stayed upon God, His peace will rule the affairs entertained by our minds. If, on the other hand, we allow our minds to dwell on the cares of this world, God's peace will be far from our thoughts. WOODROW KROLL

I have come to believe that one of the ways we can overcome the mind game of distraction is through focusing deeply on God, his Word, and his truth. I am praying that you, too, will begin to take time out of each day to enter into the presence of God. I believe this act of meditation will help bring your mind into surrender to truth. Ultimately, that's where we want our minds to drink from daily— from the truth of God.

I know that meditation is not accepted in some Christian circles today. We have images of meditation that are uncomfortable to us. We picture robed individuals sitting in the lotus position trying to find their inner selves through relaxation techniques and extreme concentration. Or we might think of those who learn meditation through mastering the precision and physicality of martial arts— karate or tae kwon do. It's difficult for many Christians to spiritually or mentally separate the act of meditation from its seemingly deeper roots in New Age communities, Hindu and Buddhist religious practices, and mystic cultures around the globe.

However, Christians who associate meditation with only Buddhism or the cultic practices of New Age mysticism are missing a rich vein of Christianity. Meditation also has deep traditional roots in Jewish and Christian history.

Scripture mentions meditation many times in both the Old and New Testaments. In fact, the book of Psalms (mostly written by King David) often speaks directly about meditation, not to mention the number of times that David describes the act of meditation in various ways. He's constantly talking about his desire to have God search his heart or about his desire to simply sit in the presence of the Lord.

But even beyond Scripture, history records the practice of Christian meditation. Many theologians and pastors believe that meditation was a common and accepted form of worship for the Christians who lived shortly after Jesus' departure from the earth. Nuns and monks during the early years of the Catholic Church utilized meditation during preparation for Mass, Holy Communion, and other sacraments. And the reformer Martin Luther wrote the following note about his personal practice: "At last, meditating day and night, by the mercy of God, I began to understand that the righteousness of God is that through which the righteous live by a gift of God, namely by faith."

Throughout Christian history, meditation has been an acknowledged form of worship, prayer, and devotion. However, despite its historical significance within both the Catholic Church and Protestant denominations, meditation is not widely practiced in our churches, and most pastors and priests do not necessarily encourage it.

But for the spiritual survival of our minds, we as Christians must refamiliarize ourselves with the art of meditation. In these times when modern life distracts us and keeps our minds busy to an unhealthy degree, now more than ever we need to hear from God.

THE MIND GAMES GET PERSONAL

Worship

by Rachel Snyder

I wonder if I should be singing in my chest voice or my head voice. Ooh, I can catch this harmony! I wonder if that's distracting to the person next to me.

Oops! He sang the wrong lyrics. He does that a lot. I wonder if he's self-conscious about that.

Is she really worshipping, or does she do that because it looks good? I'll bet she's not thinking that. I should pay attention. Focus, Rachel. Focus!

I love music. I love singing. Worst of all, I love performing.

Why worst of all? Because my head will just not shut up when I'm trying to participate in worship of a musical nature. There's so much going on—the music, the video or lyrics up on the screen, the worship band ripping into the traditional worship songs. Plus I'm concerned with how I sound, and I challenge myself to try harmonies and sing out.

What drives me crazy is that, in the middle of all this distraction and vanity, a little voice always says, "Focus, Rachel! Worship!" My heart digs into the worship experience for all of ten seconds before there's a new observation to make or a new disruption to take my train of thought off the tracks.

I've prayed about this (probably not enough). I've gone to retreats that have renewed my spirit and seemingly "fixed" my group worship issues, only to lose focus a few weeks later and end up frustrated and angry with myself for letting superficial things get between me and God.

I'd like to blame this on my short attention span. The reason I'm a journalist and not a novelist lies in the fact that sitting down to write five hundred words without losing interest is far more realistic than trying to eke out five hundred pages. Trying to concentrate on worship may just be too much to ask.

The fault could lie in the excitement of worship. How can I be expected to focus when worship has become a light show, a multimedia experience, and a concert all in one? Surely this is not my fault!

However, I have to say that years of focusing on myself—how I sound, how I look, my perception of others, me, me, me—is a part of my former life that I have yet to give over to God. It's difficult to admit, but it's true.

Of all the elements of Christianity that define the lifestyle, worship is the one thing that absolutely cannot be about me. Elements like my sin and my lifestyle changes and my attitude are about me. Worship is about God—just God. It really isn't even how I feel about God. It's just about who God is. He's wonderful. He's glorious. He's powerful. He's sovereign. He's all of those things completely separate from me. If I didn't exist, he'd still be all of those things. And knowing that he's all of those things makes my distractions, my selfishness, and my excuses pretty lame.

The solution? If the singing distracts me, I can't sing—I just focus on the words and say them to God in my heart. If the light show distracts me, I can't look—I'll just close my eyes and pretend it's just me and God in an empty room.

And if none of those ideas works, I'll just be grateful that I can praise and worship God in what I do all hours of the day, not just the twenty minutes I spend in worship at church. Mercifully, two of his best qualities are patience and forgiveness. *—Rachel Snyder has a BA in English that she hopes to put to good use by teaching at the high school level in the coming years. She and her husband currently reside near Akron, Ohio.*

Be strong and very courageous. Obey all the laws Moses gave you. Do not turn away from them, and you will be successful in everything you do. Study this Book of the Law continually. Meditate on it day and night so you may be sure to obey all that is written in it. Only then

> will you succeed. I command you—be strong and
> courageous! Do not be afraid or discouraged.
> For the LORD your God is with you wherever
> you go. JOSHUA 1:7-9 (NLT)

Gresham McEwen goes to graduate school at a university on the south side of London. Because he's attending a rather liberal school, Gresham often feels as if he is under attack for sharing the opposite views to most of his peers on topics like politics and religion. He sometimes feels overwhelmed by the seemingly powerful spiritual warfare that surrounds him. When he began to feel pressure, he usually walked away from the class discussions or avoided participating in the study groups.

That was his habit until he met an old preacher at a bar late one Friday evening. Gresham shared his predicament with the old man. The retired pastor told him to go home and begin meditating on what God's truth says about the issues he'd been debating. He told young Gresham to ask God to reveal himself and to give him courage to think and speak freely with his classmates and professors.

(To be continued . . .)

People meditate for different reasons. Some are seeking God for inner peace because of depression. Others need God to reveal his strength to them. Some meditate on God's word, or on songs, simply to worship him. No matter what the reason, Christians who meditate agree that it changes their spiritual lives and brings peace to their minds.

I meditate because God shows up when I do. It's not that I believe he shows up because I am in meditation, but when I'm meditating I don't overlook him, I don't miss his voice. I always hear him. Meditating makes me quiet so I can hear God speak to me. If that isn't reason enough to meditate, I don't know what is.

When Pope John Paul II died on April 2, 2005, writer and commentator Peggy Noonan spoke on *Good Morning America* about his life. Noonan was writing a book about the pope, and one of her favorite stories was about his first visit back to his native Poland in 1978. In the midst of widespread violence and the bars of communism, organizers of the event expected 100,000 people to attend. Instead, when the time came for the pope to speak, two million people were in attendance. In what Noonan calls the most loudly heard statement for freedom in the last thirty years, those two million people began chanting, "We want God, we want God, WE WANT GOD." I believe God heard their cry.

When David meditated thousands of years ago, when Martin Luther meditated in the mid-1500s, when Oswald Chambers meditated in the early 1900s, and when you and I meditate today—all of our minds are making the same resounding request: "We want God, we want God, we want God."

(Now, back to our story . . .)

After Gresham McEwen's conversation over a beer with the old preacher, he went home and did exactly what he had been told to do. He got out his notes from a sermon he had heard on the strength that comes from God. He laid those notes out on his living room floor. He began to read the verses that the man who had preached the sermon recommended. He lit a few candles. He began to cry out to God for his Word.

Gresham didn't have some magical experience. God didn't give him a prophetic word on how to handle his classmates. But what did happen was that Gresham found peace of mind through his experience of meditating. He had spent months sweating over how he should handle his situation. He'd prayed constantly for God to give him the words to say that would make his professors scratch their heads in confusion. He wanted to wow his classmates with a larger-than-life explanation of how God sees their views. But God never gave him those words. Instead, he gave him peace.

In other words, Gresham stopped playing mind games. And to him, that was victory enough.

Oswald Chambers, a well-known Christian communicator in the late nineteenth and early twentieth centuries, spoke often about Christian meditation. Some of those statements were included in his devotional *My Utmost for His Highest*. In that great book, Chambers writes, "We should more frequently allow our minds to meditate on these great, massive truths of God."

When Chambers mentioned the "massive truths of God," he was referring to Christ's blood sacrifice, the spirit of God living in the souls of believers, and specifically about 1 John 1:7, which instructs us to "walk in the light, as he is in the light" (NIV).

During a time when choir practice and potlucks were given more thought than the idea of meditating on the good things of God, Chambers challenged his audience with an unpopular idea. He said that our spiritual lives depend on our willingness to surrender our minds to meditation. He said, "Allow [God] to be the source of all your dreams, joys and delights, and be careful to go and obey what He has said."**

Chambers was right. We should meditate in order to fully understand and comprehend the things of Jesus. When we set our minds on the things of God, we begin to understand how vast his mercies are. We're able to truly connect with his Spirit when we meditate on his greatness. In Psalms, David implies that he can't even begin to comprehend God's greatness unless God searches David's heart and mind. In chapter 139, David's basically saying, "God, you are Lord of the mornings, the God of the late nights, God of the tall mountains and the deep seas. You who are the God of all these, be my God. I can't fathom your heights or your depths; there are things about you I cannot begin to realize. Oh God, search me."

David certainly seemed to believe, as did Oswald Chambers, that God searches our hearts when we meditate on him and his attributes and that the practice of meditation draws us closer to God.

In a modern world full of distractions, focusing deeply on God is the key to a mind that is truly free.

** Oswald Chambers, *My Utmost for His Highest,* (Discovery House) Jan. 9 and Feb. 20.

manipulation

WHEN OUR MINDS ARE NOT PURSUING GOD-INSPIRED FREETHINKING,
WE CAN DO GREAT HARM TO OTHER PEOPLE. I CALL THESE INSTANCES
"LITTLE MOMENTS OF TERRORISM." I KNOW IT'S A BIT EXTREME; IT'S AN UGLY
THOUGHT BUT TRUE NONETHELESS. WE'RE TERRORISTS. WHEN OUR
TEMPERS FLARE UP OR WHEN WE MANIPULATE OTHERS OR WHEN WE ARE
UNKIND, WE BRING OUR OWN FORM OF TERROR INTO A SITUATION. SURE,
NO ONE DIES. NO ONE ENDS UP BLOODY AND IN THE HOSPITAL. NEVER-
THELESS, OUR WORDS OR ACTIONS LEAVE BEHIND A DISASTER THAT
SOMEONE HAS TO CLEAN UP.

Meet Adam Jackson. Three years ago, Adam was a very angry person. His parents were getting divorced after thirty-two years of marriage. Compounding his feelings about his parents' separation was the fact that only two weeks prior to Mom and Dad's big announcement, he'd found out that his girlfriend of two-and-a-half years was cheating on him. It certainly seemed that Adam's anger had reason.

One month later, Adam, who was twenty-six at the time, flew home to spend Christmas with his mother at their old home in New

Orleans. Just walking into the house made his blood boil. Every memory he had of growing up there now seemed pointless and untrue. After only an hour and a half of small talk, he and his mother began fighting.

"DO YOU THINK GOD IS PLEASED WITH THIS DECISION?" Adam screamed, walking out of the living room and into his old bedroom.

"Adam, don't you think I've already thought about that? I've thought about that for the last fifteen years, Son." His mother was calmer but still heated.

"OH, GREAT. IS THAT YOUR WAY OF TELLING ME YOU'VE BEEN FEELING THIS WAY SINCE I WAS A KID? SO, WHY DIDN'T YOU LEAVE US THEN, MOM? HUH?"

"ADAM, YOU DON'T UNDERSTAND," his mother replied. Trying to stay calm, she lowered her voice again. "You don't understand."

"That's where you're wrong, Mom. I do understand. I understand that you walked out on Dad after he WORKED HIS TAIL OFF FOR YOU for thirty-two years, and I won't EVER forgive you for that. I'm leaving; I gotta get out of here." He grabbed his coat and swore at his mom as he walked out the front door, slamming the door behind him. Still seething, he drove back to the airport and flew home.

Christmas was ruined. Adam's mom was crushed. Adam was depressed. He wasn't thinking free.

Journal Entry: SEPTEMBER 11, 2002

We're remembering the one-year anniversary of September 11 today. . . . Terrorism is such a strange concept to understand. But I've learned over this past year that I am a terrorist of sorts, too. Oh, I don't throw bombs and fly planes into large

buildings, but with my thoughts and words I can cause a
pretty major disaster. . . .

confessions of a strange mind

it boggles my mind to comprehend the devastation i am capable
of leaving in my path. in all honesty, it dumbfounds me to see how
my mind affects the people around me. my mind is sick sometimes.
and when my mind is sick, the sickness that is welling up inside
my brain usually ends up hurting other people. in fact, sometimes
my mind is flat-out deadly. in the past, i've hurt too many people to
count, really. i've yelled and screamed at my parents. i've created
mountains out of molehills with my sisters. i've talked about my
friends behind their backs. i've gossiped about coworkers to other
coworkers. i've spent time complaining about my church to other
attendees. i called an ex-girlfriend an obscenity. i've argued with my
wife over silly and stupid topics. i've been so angered by someone's
actions toward me that i've plotted and planned how i can retaliate
and make life a living hell for that person who hurt me. my mind has
spent a lot of time manipulating, scheming, and strategizing the best
and most effective ways to make myself feel better by hurting some-
one else. and i could continue on and on making these confessions
about how my actions have hurt the people i know, but i think you
get the point. . . .

Meet Caroline Franz, a twenty-six-year-old college graduate who
works for a leading public relations firm in Los Angeles. Today,

Caroline is happy in her life with God, but that has not always been the case. A California girl who grew up in church, she knows God's house better than most people. She walked the aisle to receive Jesus as her Savior when she was eight years old, but by the time she graduated from college, she didn't like Christians anymore. She says that her most painful memories were rooted in the church and how other Christians treated her after her unplanned pregnancy. Don't misunderstand; she says she still loved God and Jesus and all that during this time, but most Christians made her sick to her stomach.

"I went through a time in my life when I hated the idea of organized religion. This thought process not only hurt me, but it hurt many people around me. You see, I didn't keep my mouth closed about my feelings. I shared my disgust for most churches and Christians with anyone who would listen. When someone would tell me they were a Christian, I would instantly prejudge them. That attitude gave me many chances to defame Christians in front of other people. One conversation in particular makes me very sad.

"My mom is not a Christian. A few years ago, she was going through a very rough time, and during that time she began attending a church here in L.A. I hated the church she was attending. They seemed to be judgmental and harsh in their teaching. As soon as I heard about Mom's decision to go there, I freaked out. I told her all about my feelings regarding this church. I told her some of my experiences. To make a long story short, she stopped going. At the time, I was happy about her decision not to go. But today, she's still not a Christian, and I feel like my attitude might have prohibited the Spirit of God from working in her life."

Conversation with my therapist-slash-friend

"So, Matthew, what are your thoughts on church?"

"What about church?"

"I just want to know what you think about church in general."

"Honestly, I hate church. I've probably been hurt more in church than anywhere else."

"I swear. Why is it I can't ask you one simple question without opening up this huge can of worms?"

"Hey, I'm just being honest, Bill. I've had some rough church experiences, that's all."

"Do you have any happy memories from church?"

"Sure, the last time I went was a happy memory."

"How so?"

"Cuz it was the last time I went."

"Wow, Matthew, the next church that gets you is going to be quite lucky."

"Why do you say that?"

"Because you are a bitter, poor soul in need of Jesus' healing, that's why!"

"I see where you're going with this; you're trying to get me to go back to church by using reverse psychology—you're trying to make me think the church would actually desire to have me come back. That's what you're doing, isn't it?"

"Whatever you say, Matthew. Whatever you say."

"It's working; I like being needed."

"Yep; we all do."

So Caroline reacted out of her own anger toward the church and to Christians, and she emotionally manipulated her mother in a certain way. Today she's afraid her manipulations may have prevented her mother from meeting Jesus.

I'm sure that God can overcome that, but Caroline's story is just one of many I've heard. All of us have stories. All of us have things in our lives that make our minds crazy. All of us have opened our mouths and shared these feelings. Whether we think it's just harmless gossip or just a little argument, so often these actions have big ramifications that we don't know about until it's too late.

{
MY DEFINITION: manipulating

Using anything and everything you've got to maneuver people's emotions, feelings, thinking, and lives in a direction that betters your own situation.

Helen's parents began spoon-feeding her Christianity when she was two years old. She can't remember a day in her life when she didn't hear the name Jesus used fondly in her home. From day one, her family was one of the most involved families in the church. Her dad was a deacon. Her mom was a Sunday school teacher. Helen sang in the choir, worked with the kids' ministry, and was active in her youth group. In the minds of those in the church, she did everything "right."

Helen and I went to college together; we met on the very first day in a statistics class. While in college, Helen flourished like never before. She was on a leadership team for nearly every campus ministry, volunteered at her church, and sang in a praise and worship band. She was the epitome of what many thought a "good" college girl should be. (I thought she was headed for a spiritual overdose.)

On the day we graduated, she looked at me and said, "Jesus is *so* good, Matthew. I have already been offered a job at a major music label; I can't wait to begin serving Jesus through the marketing of Christian music." I was always a little jealous of Helen; life for her seemed to be so easy, so complete, so fantastic.

After college, we lost touch. Once in a while, I would hear rumors of her success through a mutual friend. I'd see her name in press releases and read about her business savvy in industry magazines. By everything I read, she was going places. Then, a few years back, I ran into Helen at her *new* job: She was a hostess at a bar/restaurant.

"HELEN!!! I'm *Matthew Turner* from *Belmont*. Do you remember me?" I asked with exuberance. "It's so great to see you! It's been *so* long."

"Hi," she said quite unexcitedly.

I could instantly tell that she didn't want to chitchat with me. In fact, she didn't even want to look at me. Her gaze pointed downward toward her feet.

"I didn't know you worked here," I said, trying not to sound too surprised. "The last time I heard, you were heading up some big marketing team at a Christian music label."

"Yeah, well, Christians suck, Matthew," she snapped. "Believe me, I learned that the hard way. I don't believe I will ever have any use for a church again—in this lifetime, anyway. . . . Do you want smoking or non?"

About six months later, I got together with Helen over coffee. She talked candidly about her feeling that for most of her life Christians had manipulated her into thinking a particular way. "I told God the other day that I was not playing games with him anymore; he was going to have to come to me," she said flamboyantly. It kind of irritated me. After she spoke for what seemed like forever, I responded.

"Helen, who do you manipulate?"

"No one. I hate manipulation. So I *never* do it."

"Of course you do. You manipulate. We all do."

"No, I don't. I don't manipulate."

"Helen, all of us manipulate. All of us have quirks in our behavior where we try to use our opinions and stories and whatever else to influence the lives of our friends and family."

"Well, that might be true for you, but I'm being honest; I don't do that."

"Helen, you're trying to manipulate yourself into believing what's coming out of your mouth right now. . . . *And* your little statement about God a few minutes ago was *complete* manipulation."

Helen just looked at me for a second. She put her hands around her coffee mug, lifted it to her mouth, and took a sip.

"I'm not trying to be mean, Helen," I said, watching as she contemplated my words. "I just want you to see yourself for who you really are. . . . Yes, the church sucks sometimes. Yes, your parents hurt you on many occasions. But you're only using those things to make excuses for yourself. And you're letting the pain cause you to go around and try to make everybody have a good opinion of *you*. I see it today. I saw it six months ago. Instead of just letting people decide what they think about you, you're trying to manipulate them into thinking that you're okay, that you're cool, that you have reason to be mad, or whatever. And sadly, you're doing the same thing to God."

Unfortunately, the last I heard, Helen is still playing mind games.

Manipulation is basically *not* being satisfied with your own life, so you do whatever you can to influence, ruin, and change the lives of your friends and family. You do these things in hopes of controlling their situation, or perhaps it's because you want to make your situation seem better. In the end, manipulators, unless they are on soap operas, *always* end up stinking.

It doesn't have to be this way. Our minds don't ever have to hurt people. When someone is freethinking, he or she makes a point to put those harmful thoughts and potentially dangerous actions into the hands of God. It's not a simple task to leave your anger and malice in God's hands, but if you do, you'll free up your mind to focus more on the things of value and on the things in life that truly matter. Jesus talks plainly about this in the Sermon on the Mount. He said that if we are angry with our brother, we are guilty of murder. He said that when we are harmed by other people, we shouldn't retaliate; instead, we should love our enemies. But being kind and loving and peaceful when our minds are filled with frustration and doubt and anger is quite difficult.

It's true that life fills up our minds. Actually, that's an understatement. You get fired from your job and instantly you're wishing all kinds of ludicrous things would happen to your former employer. Your parents get divorced and you're suddenly mad as fire about having to split Christmases and Thanksgivings between two households. You're feeling overwhelmed by your schoolwork, working two jobs to get by, and living in a three-bedroom house with five people, and suddenly you feel anxious and irritable. These are the kinds of situations that life brings. We all have moments and events in our lives that send our hearts and minds into a frenzy. Some of us will face bigger situations than others. But Jesus doesn't leave us empty-handed. He always gives us a way out. And what I love about the truth of God, what I love about pursuing freethinking is this: The same power that resurrected Jesus from the dead is what will pull us through the sickness, the death, the overwhelming circumstances, the divorce, and all the other things that fill our minds up to the brim. That same power resides within all who know Jesus.

I experienced a devastating Memorial Day weekend three years ago. A cousin died of an aneurysm on Friday, a musician friend died in a car accident on Saturday, and a kid who worked for me commited suicide on Monday. That was the holiday weekend from hell. I was numb. My mind was so full and I was feeling so many different things that I could hardly communicate. It wasn't until I got through all the funerals and visitations and crying sessions that I truly had a moment to realize what had just happened.

I could have gotten angry with God; I could have taken that anger out on other people. But I made a conscious decision not to be bitter. It wasn't some glorious God moment where I felt him touch my life and all of a sudden I had all the answers I was looking for. I simply told God that I didn't understand the *why* behind all of this, but I knew the *who* that stood with me through it all. And with that, I surrendered my thoughts and my thinking about my circumstances over to his keeping. And I don't mean to seem cocky, but I was able to walk through that situation peacefully because I gave God the thoughts that were rushing through my mind.

Giving God our hard circumstances requires us to believe that God is good. We can't just know it; we must believe it, too. When our best friend dies in a car accident, God is still good. When our father is battling alcoholism, God is still good. When our spouse is trying her hardest to beat cancer, God is still good. We will not always understand God's goodness, but in order for us not to let our minds become overwhelmed with anger, sadness, depression, and the like, we must believe he is good. Having faith that he is good is the first step toward letting him have the hard circumstances of our lives. When we surrender the hard stuff over to his will, we are making a giant leap toward freethinking.

> For I hear the slander of many; there is terror on every side; they conspire against me and plot to take my life. But I trust in you, O LORD; I say, "You are my God." PSALM 31:13-14 (NIV)

Jesus was quite clear on the topic of terrorism. He said to love your enemies. He said to pray for those who persecute you. He said to turn the other cheek. He said to repay evil with good. And even though these are hard concepts for the majority of us to understand, Jesus expects us to do these things whether our minds are peaceful or alarmed, clear or ransacked with clutter. He didn't say "*If* things are going well for you, treat other people kindly. In fact, he said the opposite: "If people are doing all kinds of evil against you, repay that evil with good."

Getting to the place where we treat people with the love and respect that Jesus expects of us often starts in the mind. Our brains handle the information we receive either healthily or unhealthily. In other words, we're either using the information as fuel to wage war against humanity or we're mentally placing those things in the hands of God and letting him retaliate if he wants to. We have to choose the latter.

I ran into Adam Jackson a few weeks before finishing this book. We talked for a while about his reaction to his parents' splitting up.

"It's been three years since my parents got divorced," he said. "And today, I'm a lot better than I was back then; I had to give it to God by putting the pain and anger in his hands. Matthew, I was a very sick person at that time. I hurt my mom badly. But we've since gotten things straight; life is okay. I mean, it's still really weird spending holidays split up, but I had to give my thoughts about that over to God, too."

"Sounds like you've learned a lot through this," I said.

"Oh, you have no idea. My mind was literally making me go crazy. Thankfully, I was weak enough to just surrender it. It's still a battle, but I am *so* much stronger for being weak."

Is world peace even possible? Maybe the question has been pitched to you, too. I usually laugh and say, "I don't know if world peace is possible, but 'situational peace' is always possible." I believe it's possible if one person makes the choice to take the high road and respond with a "soft answer" or a "turned cheek" instead of responding with all that might be rushing through his or her mind.

Whether or not you consider yourself a terrorist, you can probably recall situations in your life where you tossed a little bomb or used a verbal machine gun instead of peacefully representing Christ. But when Jesus reigns supreme in our minds, we hand over the authority, the bombs, the guns—all our methods of war—and place them in his care.

When we let God have our minds, through prayer, through meditation, through consciously handing him control, he comes inside with all his miraculous power and renews us. And it's that renewal that readies us for our next encounter with the person we've spent a lot of time hating. But instead of hating, instead of throwing a bomb, we are peaceful, loving, unselfish, and gracious toward our "enemies." This is the kind of freethinking that changes the reality of our days. And when you see the power of God changing your circumstances from bad to good, from okay to great—it makes you want to keep surrendering your mind over to his will.

The mind is powerful, but it is even more powerful when it's resting in the hands of God.

C H A P T E R   8

surrender

When you get to a place in life where your story is no longer your story, you're close to surrender. Surrender is about being dependent. It's about being engaged. It's about not being the main character of your personal story. In fact, it's about not being a character at all. It's about becoming a part of God's story. That's surrender.

Journal Entry: May 3, 2003

I feel more peaceful today than I have felt in years. . . .

Every one of us walks around with different thoughts running through our heads. Each of our minds figures and calculates those thoughts differently. All of us have various problems that we have to work through. Some of us struggle with codependence. Others are depressed and stressed and overworked. Some of us are doubtful and cynical. Others are angry and emotionally explosive. We think these thoughts, feel these emotions, and experience these things in different ways.

The way we think affects every aspect of our lives.

A lot can be said for the way we think. Napoleon Hill, the renowned motivational speaker and writer, certainly believed in the power of thinking. He said, *"You are searching for the magic key that will unlock the door to the source of power; and yet you have the key in your own hands, and you may use it the moment you learn to control your thoughts."* Hill no doubt had different ideas on how to control one's thoughts than the average God-follower, but he still believed that much of our life is controlled by how we think.

The point I'm getting to is this: Each of us has a big life story we carry with us daily. That story affects the way we think. How we *think* about that story, how we react to that story, affects the way we live. But despite how differently each person's mind might work, despite how big or small our stories might be, despite how healthy or unhealthy our minds are—each of our stories leads us to one conclusion: All of us are in desperate need for God to consistently and often intervene on our behalf.

Our minds' need for God probably seems overtly obvious to many. But I know that throughout my life, my mind has needed to be reminded again and again of its need for God. I forget sometimes how much I need him. It's not on purpose, but sometimes the busyness of life causes me to find solace and security in my own thinking—not because I believe my thoughts are good, but because I sometimes am selfishly intrigued by my thoughts *because they are mine.*

But I've learned over the years that no matter how many times we give our minds over to God, or meditate on his truth, or pursue a life of surrender, the truth is that we will sometimes try to do things our own way. We continually have to give God control of our minds.

I wish it weren't that way, but freethinking isn't a magic formula that you drink once and never have to think about again. Our minds don't work like that. Freethinking takes hard work and determination. We're not going to just "get it" and suddenly be free. Freethinking is a progressive journey—we pick up truths along the way. But the most important ingredient for freethinking is grace— because when life throws us curves, our minds must cling to God's promise that his grace is sufficient.

> Each time he [the Lord] said, "My gracious favor is all you need. My power works best in your weakness." So now I am glad to boast about my weaknesses, so that the power of Christ may work through me. 2 CORINTHIANS 12:9 (NLT)

You've heard the old adage, "When life brings you lemons, make lemonade." I happen to think this is a very silly cliché. Maybe it's because I don't know how to make very good lemonade. The lemonade I make always ends up tasting sour or too watered down or bitter. And really, where are you supposed to get the sugar when the only thing life has brought you is a bunch of lemons? My logic tells me that I'd rather just hold on to those lemons. And when life finally decides to give me a tall glass of sweet iced tea, I'll put them in the tea. But as silly as this little cliché is, as pointless as it really is, people in Christian circles use it a lot. And even if we don't use the actual saying, the advice tends to be the same.

We're a people who tend to make the answers to our problems too simple. Christianity is full of people who tell us to work through our head problems. We're often told to pray harder and to have more faith. This advice typically comes from the kinds of people who seem to think they have all the answers. I've met people like this more than a few times in my life. When you're dealing with the mind, you hardly need a clichéd or formulaic answer.

Blaine Rochester was a Bible study leader for a young adult study group at a church I used to go to. He was a nice guy. He knew Scripture better than most assistant pastors I knew. But there was harshness in the advice Blaine handed out that I never quite understood.

One time I was having a little bit of a crisis and the head pastor of my church said I should meet with Blaine to discuss my dilemma. So I did. We had lunch and talked about my anxiety disorder. My conversation with him was interesting to say the least.

After ordering our food, we had a little small talk. Blaine showed me a couple of pictures of his two little ones . . . but then the conversation went like this:

"Blaine, I think I have a problem," I said with obvious hesitation in my voice. I wasn't sure I wanted to be telling him my life story. But the pastor had told me to, so I kept working through it. "I think I have a problem with anxiety. I'm always anxious, man. I've been waking up in the middle of the night with panic attacks. I'm not able to remain concentrated on one particular topic or job at work. I'm hardly sleeping. I think there's something in my head that's not quite balanced. I'm actually considering going on medication."

"Are you really?" He sounded disappointed, like I had just told him I had a major cocaine problem. "Where's your faith in God, Matthew? God doesn't want us dependent on medications."

"Where's my *faith*? You're questioning my faith in God because I am considering going on meds to treat my anxiety? How did I know that you would respond this way?"

"Matthew, everybody's going on medication these days. People think medication will solve their problems. I don't think it's the answer *most of the time.*"

"And you base this theory on what, Blaine? Please tell me if your theory has any biblical backing. I really want to know." I asked all these questions, but inside I was trying hard to stay calm. (I wanted so badly to be a *terrorist* at that particular moment and give him a piece of my mind.)

"Well, God expects his followers to trust him, and sometimes trusting him requires us not to jump haphazardly into poor choices. Just my opinion, Matthew, but I believe strongly that meds for emotional issues are a big mistake."

"Blaine, what do you say to the person who is in the middle of cancer treatment?"

"That's very different; that's a *real* problem."

"So, because *you* deem anxiety or depression not real, then it must be a sin to even consider taking meds to treat such disorders. I've never heard anything so ridiculous in all my life. We should probably talk about something else. . . ."

"Matthew, just pray long and hard before you make this decision, okay?"

Blaine's reaction made me feel like I was Moses and I had just struck the rock instead of simply speaking to it like God had commanded. He made me feel like I was about to commit a huge act of disobedience. Why my pastor would have recommended that I talk to Blaine about my anxiety I will never know.

After that conversation, many questions ran through my head: *Does my pastor also think I shouldn't go on meds? Is that why he sent me to Mr. Anti-therapist Blaine? Is there somewhere in the Bible where*

Jesus preached against psychiatric meds? Does God hate that I'm antide-
pressant bound? I wonder if he minds the fact that it was my mom's idea?
What the heck should I do?

The next week, I nervously walked into my doctor's office. I told
him everything I was feeling and experiencing. I told him about the
panic attacks. I told him about my inability to stay focused on one
thing for any length of time. I told him that sometimes I have extreme lows followed by extreme highs.

He prescribed Zoloft.

I never thought that my problem with anxiety would necessitate
medication. Honestly, I hated the fact I was being put on medication. For a long time, I had been one of those people (just like
Blaine) who resisted the idea of going on meds to help me cope. But
I was struggling, and I needed to do something drastic.

I struggled with a lot of questions: *Does the fact that I'm going on*
medication mean I am not surrendering? Does it mean that I am not focus-
ing enough on truth? Am I letting the mind games win? Is this really the
right thing for me?

Probably like many Christians who make a decision to take anti-
depressants, I worried what God might think. But through that time
of questioning, I learned that a big part of surrendering and freethinking is allowing grace to move in, through, and around every situation. God is a gracious God. His grace abounds more than we will
ever know and understand. I've stopped trying to grasp God's grace
because it's too broad and deep and vast for a human mind to even
begin to comprehend.

So, with my decision to go on Zoloft, I let go of all my preconceived thoughts and trusted that God, no matter his ultimate
thinking about medications for the mind, would let his grace reign
within me.

A mind set free by God's grace will fly. Through every battle I have ever fought inside my head, I have always clung to that theory. I've had some grandiose moments when that statement rang true in my life. The moments when I surrender my thoughts over to God are the moments I really learn about what it means to have faith. You see, I believe that many of the huge accomplishments by people in Scripture weren't necessarily big leaps for their hearts and souls—I believe they were big leaps of faith for their *minds*. Like I've noted throughout this book, it's our minds that are often the last part to jump on board with believing, surrendering, and free-thinking.

When Moses saw the burning bush and heard the voice of God come from it, I can only imagine that his heart and soul jumped at the chance to believe he was communing with Almighty God. But his mind probably questioned, "Hey, who is this? Is this *really* God?" David obviously worked through many doubts on his way to believing wholeheartedly in the power of God. Think about it! Jacob wrestled. Elisha pouted. Solomon asked. These men had real questions; their minds struggled with belief. The same is true for Peter. When he took that first step onto the choppy surface of the water, it was his heart's love for Jesus that made him get out of the boat. But as soon as his mind caught up with what his heart was doing, into the water he fell.

God is used to dealing with our fragile minds. He's not surprised by our inability to fully understand him, so his patience and grace is great for those of us who struggle to get our heads to follow suit in our journey of faith.

Last year, I met a young man named Dale, a writer for his university newspaper. He contacted me because I had written a feature for a magazine about my battle with depression and anxiety. He wanted to do a story on me. He was in my town for a wedding, so we set up a time to meet for coffee. It was this interview that led me to write this book. The following is the edited interview:

Q: Matthew, I've read a couple of your books. But when I read the article about depression, I was somewhat dumbfounded by your honesty, as a Christian, to admit that you struggle. How did you get to a place where you could be so honest about your problem?

A: Aren't Christians supposed to be honest? Because seriously, admitting I had a problem was really the easy part. The hard part for me came in finding out how I was going to work through my problem. Most of the time, certainly not always, it's easy for me to share where I am on my life's journey.

Q: When did you first think you had a problem?

A: I actually don't remember *ever* thinking I was completely normal. Even as a child, I was always the kid who was just a little bit different from everybody else. But I think I really began to see a problem with anxiety my first year out of college. That's when I first battled codependency—or at least that's when I began to recognize it in my life.

Q: Were you able to talk to your family about it right away?

A: Well, my mom is a psychiatric nurse, so talking to her about it was rather easy. We talked at length about it when I first began identifying the symptoms in my life. Although my father was less open about the topic, even he was patient and understanding of my circumstance. But my mom and I talked at length about what I was feeling—the loneliness, the stress, the panic attacks, the fear. For many years, Mom was my therapist.

Q: Did your attacks keep getting worse?

A: They did. I would actually go for months when I would not see any symptoms of depression or anxiety, but then I would have a bout that would last a week. Those prolonged bouts got closer and closer as time went on. Eventually, I was having a bad week every two or three weeks. And, of course, as I got older I was more aware of my symptoms. I was able to recognize my flaws much faster than before.

Q: What did you do first to try to remedy your problem?

A: I prayed a lot.

Q: Did that work?

A: Sure, sometimes. I mean, God always heard my requests, and sometimes he would deliver me from my battles. But anxiety and depression are disorders that require *a lot of things* in life to work together in order for healing to occur. It's not just about emotional or mental healing—healing begins when our entire person falls in line. Don't get me wrong; I believe God could have chosen to heal me of my depression—you know, like one big miraculous happening. But I had to learn that instant miracles are not always on his agenda. Sometimes we learn more by walking through a long, painful process of healing.

Q: When did healing begin?

A: I guess healing *began* when I started handing over major parts of my life to Christ. Surrender is a process, but it is also a war that rages hard inside our minds. It's not a one-battle war. I would give up, then take back, then give up again, and take back again. It was quite a process.

Q: What was the most difficult part of the healing?

A: Trusting. Getting to a place in my life where I was able simply to trust God with the different emotions and fears and symptoms that I was feeling was sometimes very hard. When you're right in the middle of feeling utterly depressed or overwhelmed by the hell that codependency puts you through, it's hard to just give that up when your mind is telling you to be consumed by it.

Q: When did full surrender of your mind finally happen?

A: You know, Dale, full surrender happens as often as it needs to happen—sometimes it's daily or hourly or minute by minute. I have gotten to a place where I have to constantly pursue surrender. I must always keep my mind in a place where it is ready, willing, and able to surrender to God's ultimate purpose at any moment.

Q: When you surrender, what are you hoping will happen?

A: I'm hoping to be free. I'm hoping to think with the confidence and peace and hope that Jesus says comes when I follow him. I had a friend who called this phenomenon *freethinking*. And through life, I have learned that there is a process to freethinking. We first have to come to a point where we realize that God wants our minds. And once we get there, he begins to teach us the character of a mind fully reliant on him. That kind of mind relies on truth, isn't codependent, and engages life fully and purely.

In my further conversation with Dale, as he began to talk about his own battles of the mind and battles that he's seen his friends fighting, I realized that maybe a lot of other people were struggling with similar issues to the ones I have struggled with. Out of this realization came the idea—a prompting from God, I believe—to write *Mind Games*.

Surrendering my heart to God was the beginning of my relationship with him. And that part (at least, for me) was rather easy. However, it was only the beginning. As I grew closer to God, as I got to know him as my Father, my Savior, and my counselor, he started asking me for more and more of myself. He also wanted my sexuality, my passions, my desires, my fears. And my mind.

I was quick to surrender most of these things—at least verbally. But when he asked for my mind, I said no. Well, I didn't actually say, "No!," but I thought it—loudly. And God heard me every time.

I believe the mind is always the hardest entity to hand over to God. Why? Because doing so requires us to surrender how we think, what we think, and what we believe to be true. Let's face it, thinking is quite important to us. We pride ourselves on being able to rationalize and decide for ourselves. We like being able to make big decisions and to believe in our hearts that life is in our control. To give up our minds is to give up how we think. For a long time, I couldn't do that. I thought, *God has everything else, why does he want my mind?*

Obviously, I was naive. At the time, I did not know that my mind was so connected to my heart, my sexuality, my desires, my passions, and my fears. I didn't realize that my mind touched every aspect of my life. But, thankfully, God woke me up. And now, at least for today, he has my mind.

I've come to realize that it's impossible for God to have my entire heart if he doesn't have my mind. And it's impossible for him to have my passions if he doesn't have my mind. Although the heart and soul represent the core of who we are, our minds influence our hearts and souls to be what they are.

If we haven't given God our minds, he will keep pursuing us until we do.

Surrender is the key. And giving God our minds is not a one-time handover of power, either. It's a weekly, daily, hourly, and minute-by-minute kind of surrender. Every day, I must wake up and ask

God to take control of my mind, or I will quickly take it back into my own hands.

I don't know about your hands, but my hands are dirty.

It's true that all of us struggle with different mental battles. It's true that all of us get up in the morning and have different thoughts that provoke and challenge us. In other words, we all play different mind games. But as different as we are, if we pursue freethinking, if we pursue a mind set on Christ, we will be set free.

Are you ready to surrender? Freethinking begins with giving everything to God.

peace

"Those who think they can do it on their own end up obsessed with measuring their own moral muscle but never get around to exercising it in real life. Those who trust God's action in them find that God's Spirit is in them—living and breathing God! Obsession with self in these matters is a dead end; attention to God leads us out into the open, into a spacious, free life. Focusing on the self is the opposite of focusing on God. Anyone completely absorbed in self ignores God, ends up thinking more about self than God. That person ignores who God is and what he is doing. And God isn't pleased at being ignored."

Romans 8:5-8 ("The Message")

Freethinking begins with surrender. Surrender daily. Surrender passionately. Surrender now. The first step is hard, but it will change the rest of your life.

"I am leaving you with a gift—peace of mind and heart.
And the peace I give isn't like the peace the world gives.
So don't be troubled or afraid." John 14:27 (NLT)

The classics.

Love 'em,

hate 'em,

avoid 'em like the plague.

Most of us fit into one of these categories when it comes to stuff written a long time ago in lands far, far away by people named St. Augustine, St. Teresa, or Brother Lawrence.

But you'd be surprised at how similar their questions and struggles are to what we're dealing with today. Just like us, they loved, doubted, failed, and grew. And in the midst of all of it, they took a chance on following God and were absolutely blown away by the results!

Now it's your turn to be blown away. This book contains the revolutionary ideas of twenty of the most influential Christian thinkers and writers of all time. And their messages are as relevant today as they were decades and, in some cases, centuries ago.

Yep. These are definitely twenty of our favorites. Hopefully they'll become some of yours as well.

Pick up your copy of *Twenty Things You Should Read* at a bookstore near you!

Available now!

- Get a job
- Pay the rent
- Find a church
- Go to the gym
- Call Mom and Dad
- Pick up dry cleaning
- Return videos

u want a life of purpose and meaning.
u've got the passion.
t who's got the time?

ɔm defining your relationships and
naging your money and career to
engthening your faith and under-
nding the culture around you, *Every-
ɩg Twentys* will help you make the
st of the best decade of your life!

< up a copy of *Everything Twentys* today!
ilable now at a bookstore near you.